Small Shifts,
MEANINGFUL
IMPROVEMENT

·····

Small Shifts,
MEANINGFUL IMPROVEMENT

Collective Leadership Strategies for Schools and Districts

·····

P. Ann Byrd
Alesha Daughtrey
Jonathan Eckert
Lori Nazareno

·····

Arlington, Virginia USA

2800 Shirlington Road, Suite 1001 • Arlington, VA 22206 USA
Phone: 800-933-2723 or 703-578-9600 • Fax: 703-575-5400
Website: www.ascd.org • Email: member@ascd.org
Author guidelines: www.ascd.org/write

Richard Culatta, *Chief Executive Officer;* Anthony Rebora, *Chief Content Officer;* Genny Ostertag, *Managing Director, Book Acquisitions & Editing;* Susan Hills, *Senior Acquisitions Editor;* Mary Beth Nielsen, *Director, Book Editing;* Liz Wegner, *Editor;* Thomas Lytle, *Creative Director;* Donald Ely, *Art Director;* Bailey Gregory/The Hatcher Group, *Graphic Designer;* Circle Graphics, *Typesetter;* Kelly Marshall, *Production Manager;* Shajuan Martin, *E-Publishing Specialist*

All web links in this book are correct as of the publication date below but may have become inactive or otherwise modified since that time. If you notice a deactivated or changed link, please email books@ascd.org with the words "Link Update" in the subject line. In your message, please specify the web link, the book title, and the page number on which the link appears.

PAPERBACK ISBN: 978-1-4166-3236-8   ASCD product #123007   n9/23
PDF EBOOK ISBN: 978-1-4166-3237-5; see Books in Print for other formats.
Quantity discounts are available: email programteam@ascd.org or call 800-933-2723, ext. 5773, or 703-575-5773. For desk copies, go to www.ascd.org/deskcopy.

Library of Congress Cataloging-in-Publication Data

Names: Byrd, P. Ann, author. | Daughtrey, Alesha, author. | Eckert, Jonathan, author. | Nazareno, Lori, author.
Title: Small shifts, meaningful improvement : collective leadership strategies for schools and districts / P. Ann Byrd, Alesha Daughtrey, Jonathan Eckert, Lori Nazareno.
Description: Arlington, VA : ASCD, 2023. | Includes bibliographical references and index.
Identifiers: LCCN 2023019500 (print) | LCCN 2023019501 (ebook) | ISBN 9781416632368 (paperback) | ISBN 9781416632375 (pdf)
Subjects: LCSH: Teacher-administrator relationships—United States. | Professional learning communities—United States. | Educational leadership—United States. | Educational change—United States.
Classification: LCC LB2831.58 .B97 2023 (print) | LCC LB2831.58 (ebook) | DDC 371.1/06—dc23/eng/20230606
LC record available at https://lccn.loc.gov/2023019500
LC ebook record available at https://lccn.loc.gov/2023019501

The work of any team or organization needs to start with a clear sense of what they are trying to accomplish and how they want to behave together. . . . Once this clarity is established, people will use it as their lens to interpret information, surprises, experience. They will be able to figure out what and how to do their work. Their individual decisions will not look the same, and there is no need for conformity in their behavior. But over time, as the individual solutions are fed back into the system, as learning is shared, we can expect that an orderly pattern will emerge.

—Margaret Wheatley, *Leadership and the New Science*

What we need to do is learn to work in the system, by which I mean that everybody, every team, every platform, every division, every component is there not for individual competitive profit or recognition, but for contribution to the system as a whole on a win-win basis.

—W. Edwards Deming

Small Shifts, MEANINGFUL IMPROVEMENT

Collective Leadership Strategies for Schools and Districts

• • • • •

1

Collective Leadership: A Practice, Not a Program

This book is not about a *program*. Rather, it is a resource guide and a call to *practice*, meant to support leadership work that will advance how administrators and teachers collaborate, learn together, generate solutions to long-standing challenges, and make those solutions stick over time.

If you are engaged in any type of leadership work with schools, you already have more than a few programs you are trying to implement. In fact, you may be taking on more than you feel you can implement well. What you and your team need is not another thing to add to an already full plate but a way of seeing and sharing that plate differently. Maybe you even dream of taking away a thing or two so that you can unleash all your energy on what matters most to make a difference for the students and staff you serve.

These are the kinds of shifts—small, daily, practical, and powerful—that collective leadership is about. Collective leadership, which is the focus of our work at Mira Education, is not a program to implement but a set of practices through which teachers and administrators influence colleagues and others to improve teaching, learning, and innovation. Indeed, if collective leadership becomes something that people add or another program to do, then it will fail. As Matt Sherman, a principal with whom we have worked, said, "Collective leadership is not another thing to add to your plate. It *is* the plate."

For us, a main reason for shifting from leadership programs to collective leadership practice is that the programs, even ones we admire, often don't work—at least not for long. They may require expensive and time-consuming technical training, making them difficult to scale and sustain. They require perfect conditions with "rockstar" educators to get started, rather than helping leadership teams find ways to start from where they are. They require massive capacity found only in large or well-funded systems, or they oversimplify complex adaptive challenges into technical ones with silver-bullet solutions. (See "Adaptive Leadership" for more on the distinction between adaptive and technical challenges—a distinction that we will return to throughout the coming chapters.)

After working with hundreds of schools in contexts that range from large urban districts on both coasts to rural towns in South Carolina, we know that every context is different. Therefore, every improvement has to be contextualized. However, we believe that we have identified, developed, and applied a process that can be used across contexts to surface adaptive challenges in order to implement adaptive solutions. We assume that you picked up this book because you recognize that things are not what they could be in education. With a few shifts, we think that education (and your team's leadership) can deliver on its promise to each student.

Four Foundational Practices

If we are going to start making shifts as leaders, then we need to understand four foundational practices. We all share responsibility for creating teams and learning communities where educators in every role all do the following:

- Lead meaningful work.
- Retain and grow expertise.
- Prepare students for the future.
- Make collective leadership "the plate" rather than an addition to what are already full plates of work across the team.

To approach sustainability, these practices require a change in mindset. The complexity of the challenges our students face requires the collective expertise of all educators in a given context, which in turn requires leaders to retain and grow talent. To do this, collective leadership should not add to the work of overstretched educators. Instead, collective leadership is an approach that provides mutual support toward shared goals. We need adaptive leadership to create and cultivate the conditions in which educators and students can flourish.

Adaptive Leadership

Adaptive challenges (Heifetz, 1994) require a change in mindset because the problem and solution are unclear. Technical challenges, on the other hand, have clear problems and solutions. When we try to apply technical solutions to adaptive challenges, we breed frustration that can lead to cynicism among those who are entrusted with implementing the technical solutions.

Adaptive change requires adaptive leadership. Adaptive leadership of teachers and administrators focuses on improvement, habits, identity, and work. Solutions indicate finality—that a problem is solved—when we know in education that the work is too complex and iterative to be simplified as a solution (Kegan & Lahey, 2009). Our objective is to improve, which makes taking each next step less daunting because we are just getting better. We also focus on what we can do each day to get better rather than focusing on more abstract, distal goals (Clear, 2018). As we develop habits that become part of our identity, we rely less and less on self-control and more on our team and the identity we build together (Clear, 2018). We focus on *work* rather than a leadership *position* because we want individuals who have the expertise to step into leadership rather than worry about whether they have the correct position (Eckert, 2018).

This book frames a process that will support administrator and teacher development in a sustainable way. The process acknowledges that our first efforts "are possibly wrong and definitely incomplete" (Bryk et al., 2015, p. 79). Adaptive leadership is foundational to the shifts in leadership practice described throughout the book.

Lead Meaningful Work

"Collective leadership encompasses the practices through which teachers and administrators influence colleagues, policymakers, and others to improve teaching and learning" (Eckert, 2018, p. 5). Simply put, collective leadership is work toward shared goals. In schools, that means that staff, paraprofessionals, teachers, and administrators are all leading because each person is contributing work toward the shared goal of student learning. This statement is not a platitude. Our work influences others and therefore is leadership. At the same time, all leadership is not necessarily good leadership (Kellerman, 2004); therefore, we must attend to how the work that influences others is or is not leading toward positive shared goals.

Listening in on conversations in a teacher workroom is a good way to get a sense of how leadership is being enacted. Is the workroom a place where growth, success, and students are celebrated? Or is it a place where frustration, negative venting, and withering criticism reign? We lead with our words and actions.

One phrase that needs to be removed from every school leader's vernacular is "just a teacher." When teachers refer to themselves as "just a teacher," they are stripping themselves of the influence that comes with the profession that makes all others possible. When administrators, teachers, or community members use the phrase, they are also relegating teachers to low status without acknowledging the power that teachers have.

In healthy school communities, administrators, teachers, staff, and students lead with one another. Certainly, there are many decisions that administrators must manage, such as supervisory evaluations, bus routes, school maintenance, and other technical responsibilities. However, wherever possible, particularly as it relates to instruction, engaging a wide range of leaders in the building taps the collective expertise of the educator community in ways that will lead to more robust improvement. For example, one elementary school with which we work takes a two-day retreat in the spring to build its school improvement plan for the following year with a team of administrators, teachers, and two student representatives. They determine the goals for the following year based on the progress they have made on the current year's goals. Both teachers and administrators cite the inclusion of students on the team as a primary reason for the success of their award-winning school.

Retain and Grow Expertise

Finding and retaining teachers has become a significant challenge for many school districts. In addition, the pool of substitute teachers has vanished (Gecker, 2021). Districts in some states, such as California, have sent home notes in children's lunch boxes to let parents know that they are hiring teachers. Others are offering significant signing bonuses (Gecker, 2021). At the time of this writing, teacher morale was at a record low (Will, 2021). Although school leaders cannot control the cultural currents swirling around schools or the ebbs and flows of pandemics or politics, they can lead in ways that cultivate an environment where colleagues and students flourish. One of the primary reasons teachers leave the profession is the lack of support from administration (Carver-Thomas & Darling-Hammond, 2019; SC-T, 2021). Collective leadership, in its design and implementation, is dependent on and builds administrative support.

If we want to create conditions that will retain and develop the expertise among educators that our students deserve, then collective leadership is the vehicle for doing so. Instead of making teachers *feel* supported, each educator *is* supported because administrators and teachers build the school culture together by engaging in leadership work toward shared goals.

One urban high school in Illinois, a nationally recognized school for its use of Positive Behavioral Interventions and Supports (PBIS), exemplifies the kind of work that retains expertise by developing it. A special education teacher noted that the school was not effectively engaging students in a positive learning culture. He convened a team of colleagues, parents, and students to determine how the school could improve in this area. The principal was invited as a member of the team but was not the leader or even the catalyst of the work. The team meets monthly to discuss their student discipline numbers as well as the markers they have identified for progress related to school climate and culture.

In sharing power, by allowing an energized, solution-oriented teacher leader to do the work that he saw as a need, the school made remarkable improvement. The principal attended the monthly meetings and contributed where needed (and also provided snacks). The work of the PBIS team changed the school culture and made it an empirically more positive place for administrators, teachers, and students to work. Teacher retention and development occurred because of the power that teachers had to lead and own improvement work. The initiation of the work, the design of the team, and the shift in school culture all made the school a more equitable and inclusive community that identified and celebrated its individual members.

Schools do not necessarily need more team-building exercises or programs to support teacher development. Across the United States, we see that the best development that leads to retention of high-quality educators occurs through shared work that improves outcomes for students. The work they are doing together is the development experience. When both teachers and administrators share the work, they grow in competence and in understanding the work of the other. If we attend to this type of retention and development, recruitment will take care of itself because these schools and districts—and our profession—will become a desirable destination for prospective professionals.

Prepare Students for the Future

Until 1900, experts estimated that human knowledge doubled each century. By the end of World War II, they estimated that it doubled every 25 years. Now, experts believe that human knowledge doubles every 12 months (Richey, 2020). This acceleration has tremendous implications for education. We are not preparing students for a 20th-century reality; we are preparing them for an accelerating future in a constantly shifting present.

The good news is that we know more about how people learn and have more tools to deliver and assess instruction than ever before. Much of that doubling of knowledge has enhanced our ability to teach in innovative ways. Instead of fearing change, effective school leaders are embracing these tools and recognizing that the only way forward is through collective leadership with others. In an increasingly distracted and fragmented world, leadership can be more challenging, but we can build schools that offer a different approach than the ones characterized by the ALL-CAPS, divisive transactions on social media.

We are seeing schools across the United States that are building collaborative teams to solve problems that students and communities identify. For example, one middle school divides its students into houses where they study interdisciplinary problems through EL (formerly Expeditionary Learning) curriculum. On any given day, a visitor can see teams of students working in common spaces to conduct research, prepare for a debate, or create art projects incorporating recycled materials, all in the service of building stronger communities.

Students at a high school in upstate New York run a greenhouse, which they designed, that grows produce using soil and aquaponics. The greenhouse is located at a clean-water-reclamation facility. The students designed a system in which the reclaimed water flows through PVC pipes under decomposing leaves that the city collects and deposits. Through frigid winters, the decomposing leaves heat the water in the pipes to 100–110 degrees Fahrenheit. The pipes radiate enough heat to warm the greenhouse and grow plants all winter long. This one project cleans water, uses composted yard waste, and grows plants. Students refer to the class associated with the greenhouse as a "figure it out" class in which the teacher does not give students answers; instead, they work alongside research biologists to find ways to improve their systems. All students have access to these classes, not just a privileged few. Students receive the basic instruction they need in their classrooms three to four days per week and then engage with experts as their own expertise grows.

Make Collective Leadership "the Plate," Not Another Add-On

Often, new school programs fail because they are just another initiative added on top of everything else the school is already doing. Whether it is a federal, state, or local mandate, it is just another thing that educators must wedge into days that have only 24 hours.

Collective leadership allows educators to share the work in a way that builds ownership rather than buy-in. Collective leadership is more than task delegation. Collective leadership unleashes educators' collective expertise to solve problems in ways that are similar to those found in some of today's most successful companies. If there is a commonality across big technology companies, it is their relentless pursuit of feedback that they can use to improve. Whether they should or should not be collecting all of the data they have is not the point. Undeniably, they use the data to increase profit, and they get data from every available source. However, they not only collect information but also analyze, dissect, and manage it in order to maximize their performance.

Collective leadership in schools, particularly when it occurs across networks of schools, can follow similar principles. In the improvement communities we support, teams of teachers and administrators from each school work on common problems of practice. They identify the adaptive challenge they need to address and determine what observable improvement would look like. Then, at least one teacher and one administrator from each school track their data from month to month, report the data on a spreadsheet that is shared across the network, and participate in a monthly Zoom session with all the schools in the network to check progress. At the end of each year, the schools meet to showcase their improvement and identify where their work needs to go next. Some schools have been working in these networks for years. This type of disciplined inquiry is changing the way schools improve.

A Model for Collective Leadership Development

To support the four foundational practices, we need a model that illustrates the development of collective leadership (see Figure 1.1). Through years of research, tool development, and experience with schools, we have identified seven conditions that matter most (Eckert, 2018, 2019; Eckert & Butler, 2021; Eckert & Daughtrey, 2018; Smylie & Eckert, 2018). These seven conditions and their associated shifts are the basis of the next seven chapters, where

FIGURE 1.1
Collective Leadership Development Model

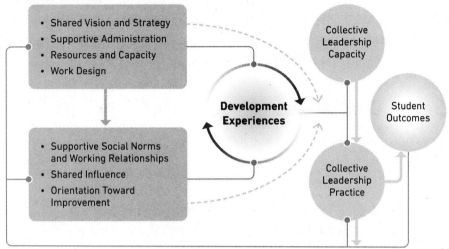

Source: From "Teaching and Leading for Exemplary STEM Learning: A Multiple-Case Study" by J. Eckert and J. Butler, 2021, *Elementary School Journal, 121*(4), p. 684. Copyright 2021 by J. Eckert and J. Butler. Adapted with permission.

they are explained in more detail. The seven conditions appear on the left side of the model, with the first four (shared vision and strategy, supportive administration, resources and capacity, and work design) influencing the other three (supportive social norms and working relationships, shared influence, and orientation toward improvement). We survey schools to determine their readiness for collective leadership and also track growth in these areas over years of engagement.

The seven conditions directly influence the development experiences that administrators and teachers share. The dotted lines in the figure illustrate how the seven conditions support or constrain the work that comes out of development experiences. For example, supportive administrators can either accelerate the good work of the team by sharing power or supporting the work coming out of the development experience. Conversely, administrators who do not trust their teams can limit the capacity for and practice of collective leadership if they undercut that work.

Effective development experiences supported by the seven conditions should establish collective leadership capacity, which then should result in improved leadership practice. As with all initiatives to help schools get better, the improved leadership practice results in enhanced student outcomes. These outcomes, in turn, strengthen leadership practice and cultivate improvement in the seven conditions. The model creates an iterative cycle of continual growth rather than a linear process.

Seven Challenges

Sometimes the easiest way to understand something is to determine what it is not. Before delving more deeply into the particulars of collective leadership, let's look at a common example from schools that should be collectively led but often are not: the professional learning community, or PLC.

Professional. Learning. Community. Shouldn't these words describe every school? "We are education professionals who facilitate and value learning in a community." So many schools embody this idea. However, in many schools *PLC* is a four-letter word. Why? Because PLCs have become something *done* to teachers instead of being a process of learning collectively that is led by the grassroots wisdom that comes from the classroom. In 2004, Rick DuFour, the educator most often associated with PLCs, wrote that a professional learning community should "focus on learning rather than teaching, work collaboratively, and hold [itself] accountable for results." At the same time, he said, the term *PLC* had "been used so ubiquitously that it is in danger of losing all meaning." Almost 20 years later, this is certainly the case in many schools.

The demise of many PLCs points to the ways in which attempts at collective leadership can founder. In the following sections, we describe the undesirable outcomes that can occur if one of the conditions of collective leadership is missing (see Figure 1.2).

Lack of Shared Vision and Strategy = Confusion

Are the vision and strategy associated with your school's approach to PLCs shared? If not, your efforts will result in confusion. We have all been on teams where the goals and strategies are unclear and we are participating in pooled ignorance, trying to figure out what administrators at the school or district level "want us to do." If you think of PLCs as a time when you meet

FIGURE 1.2

What's Missing? The Relationship Between Undesirable Outcomes and Conditions of Collective Leadership

Undesirable Outcome	Missing Condition of Collective Leadership
Confusion	Shared Vision and Strategy
Inaction	Supportive Administration
Frustration	Resources and Capacity
Lack of Sustainability	Work Design
Friction	Supportive Social Norms and Working Relationships
Burnout	Shared Influence
No Change	Orientation Toward Improvement

to go through a protocol that has to be submitted to administration, then you are lacking a shared vision and strategy. This situation not only will not lead to change but also will result in cynicism and confusion, a common outcome of insight without action.

Lack of Supportive Administration = Inaction

Most administrators we meet say a lot of things that seem to support collective leadership and PLCs. However, when the rubber meets the road or the PLC meets reality, we see wildly different levels of actual support. A few quick diagnostic questions can help determine how supportive administrators really are: *Who sets the PLC agenda? How are PLC data used? Do administrators participate as colearners in PLCs? Where do new ideas to address come from in PLCs? Do PLCs feel like partnerships or compliance-driven exercises?* Without trust, schools are unlikely to realize sustainable improvement (Bryk & Schneider, 2002). Trust, or lack thereof, becomes very evident in PLCs. Without trust and support, inaction ensues.

Lack of Resources and Capacity = Frustration

Perhaps your school has a clear vision and supportive administration, but you lack resources and human capacity for PLCs. If so, you will experience frustration. Obviously, a lack of resources to implement ideas generated by PLCs will be frustrating. Equally frustrating is lacking the capacity to actually improve as a PLC, which can happen for at least two reasons. First, your school may lack the professional talent to improve because teachers and administrators do not have the requisite skills and experience to get better— a situation that we believe is rarely the case. Second, teachers and administrators do not have any additional bandwidth because they are stretched thin in carrying out their current responsibilities. If leaders do not have the capacity to do anything more than what they are already doing, then there is little point in discussing how else they can lead without removing something from their already overflowing plates.

Lack of Intentional Work Design = Lack of Sustainability

We do not "go to" a PLC. A PLC is not merely the actual meeting time during which you "officially" collaborate. A professional learning community should be much more than a slot in a team's schedule. However, if participants do not have regular time to meet, observe one another teach, look at student work, and plan accordingly, the PLC will not be sustainable; in fact, it will never get off the ground. In schools where work design is not structured to support professional collaboration around meaningful student learning, PLCs will fail.

Lack of Supportive Social Norms and Working Relationships = Friction

It is possible for a school to adequately address the first four conditions but have social norms and relationships that are toxic. Teachers and administrators talk *about* one another instead of *to* one another. In this situation, the "crab bucket culture" (Duke, 2008) is alive and well, with teachers and administrators dragging down teachers who are recognized for success in the same way that crabs will collectively pull down any crab who might escape the bucket. Perhaps there is a sense that everyone is on their own, expected to close the classroom door and figure things out for themselves. Conversely, maybe the principal is a micromanager who is constantly engaging in leadership that undercuts the work of others. If this is the case, significant friction will emerge within and among PLCs.

Lack of Shared Influence = Burnout

Burnout ensues when there is a lack of shared influence among teachers as well as between teachers and administrators. Why? When teachers sense that they have no ability to influence or be influenced by others, they feel isolated. In a profession as challenging as education, most practitioners cannot survive the rigors of the work, day after day, without others. Those who are in the early stages of their career need support through their PLC; they cannot thrive without it. Those who have been teaching for a few years might need opportunities to lead beyond the classroom to continue to grow. Without those opportunities to lead in new ways, they also begin to shrivel professionally. A PLC should be driven by shared influence, but in those where cynicism or a compliance-driven mindset has taken root, the lack of shared influence is evident in the burnout teachers express.

Lack of Orientation Toward Improvement = No Change

Although it is hard to imagine a school that is strong in the collective leadership conditions previously described but is lacking a strong orientation toward improvement, such a situation is possible. Teachers and administrators may share a vision, support each other, be well-resourced, have strong relationships, and influence each other . . . all to maintain the status quo. In some schools where this is the case, leaders will adamantly defend their track records of success. Without the perception of significant challenges to address, they default to the notion that nothing needs to change. The PLCs in these schools are unlikely to produce any change and, in fact, might actively resist change. However, those who have spent any time in schools know that the only constant is change. To think that we have figured out how to make learning for each student meaningful is the height of hubris.

Seven Strong Conditions = Positive Impact

If PLCs effectively address all seven conditions of collective leadership, they generate positive impact. Many teachers and administrators point to PLCs as their through-line to improvement. We have observed amazing PLCs where all seven conditions are addressed and teaching and learning are constantly improving. If that is not your school, which conditions are breaking down?

Seven Conditions That Shift Schools from Program to Practice

Schools that have shifted from program to practice will understand the messy, iterative nature of collective leadership. Although the model is complex and the conditions comprehensive, we want to briefly describe each condition and direct you toward how to use this book so that it becomes part of your practice. Using the analysis tool in Figure 1.3 on page 18 may lead you to a later chapter about a condition that you need to tackle right away. Feel free to skip to that chapter based on these brief descriptions.

Shared Vision and Strategy

Talking to principals or superintendents, we can pick up pretty quickly if they really believe in a shared vision or collective leadership. If we hear a lot of personal pronouns, such as "I" or "me," or possessives such as "my team," "my school(s)," or "my staff," we have a pretty clear idea of who is at the top of the organization. In fact, the whole notion of "top" and "hierarchy" tells us a lot about the district. Is its leadership more like a web or a pyramid? Some leaders, more likely to be women, position themselves at the center of a web and build a shared vision this way. Others, more typically men, think of leadership as a pyramid with themselves at the top (Bolman & Deal, 2017), and that shared vision is something that trickles down from the top. Shared vision must, in fact, be *shared* and not something to "buy into." The approach characterized by leaders asking others to buy in insinuates that the idea is already developed and is now being sold. Collectively led, shared vision is codeveloped, co-implemented, and co-refined, and it benefits from the collective wisdom of the organization. Just as teaching is not about us as teachers, leadership is not about the leader; it is about the work that we do toward shared goals. For more insight on shared goals, see Chapter 2.

Supportive Administration

Supportive administrators act as catalysts, not micromanagers. In chemistry, a catalyst accelerates a reaction without being used up. Given all of the demands on administrators, the emphasis on not being "used up" cannot be overemphasized. Sustainable leadership requires us to act as catalysts who are not the focus of the work. Catalytic leaders support good work that is already happening or create conditions for good work to occur so that they can accelerate its impact. They draw followers to them because they advance the good work by leading beside others rather than demanding that others follow. For more information, see Chapter 3.

Resources and Capacity

Schools (and most organizations, for that matter) are limited by scarce resources. This situation is just a reality, which raises the question: How do we get more out of what we have? We are not talking about stretching people to their breaking point. Instead, we need a vision for using the resources we have in more strategic ways. How can we rethink school organization to allow time for teachers to observe one another teach and for administrators and teachers to examine student work together with the strategic goal of improving outcomes for each student? How do we maximize teaching skill and expertise within classrooms by providing opportunities for developing increased capacity in teachers and administrators? This condition is not about creating another program. It is about cultivating a learning organization that is focused on the strategic use of resources and capacity, which is the topic of Chapter 4.

Supportive Social Norms and Working Relationships

As we have said before, collective leadership is not a program, and it is certainly more than a faceless process. People develop and drive the strategies that inform the process. Trust, shared sentiment, and the disposition of confident humility (Grant, 2021) are at the core of productive working relationships and social norms. Celebrating the success of others and simultaneously owning our part of the opportunities and challenges schools face are essential to sustainable improvement. Typically, strong relationships flow from schools that have realized the conditions of shared vision and strategy, supportive administration, resources and capacity, and work structure. And, in turn, strong relationships will improve the four conditions as colleagues speak to shared vision, become supportive, use resources strategically, and express a desire to work differently. Chapter 5 explores how people, woven together in community and intricate social networks, drive the process.

Shared Influence

For too long, schools have functioned like egg cartons, siloes, or whatever metaphor we choose to indicate that educators work in isolation. Leadership is inextricably linked to influence, and shared influence leads to better outcomes. Any leadership work that does not address how to increase the benefit of influence is missing an important point. Most schools have underleveraged expertise that could bring about schoolwide improvement. How do we unleash the capacities of the third-year teacher toiling in isolation in her classroom to help others see what their students might be capable of doing? How do we create conditions where it is normal for teachers to regularly observe and give and receive feedback on their teaching? When will teachers and administrators see themselves as equal partners in the instructional leadership of schools? If your school already operates in ways that answer these three questions positively, be grateful, as yours is the exception to the rule. Chapter 6 will identify paths to creating more schools that effectively spread the expertise and influence of educators.

Orientation Toward Improvement

Improvement happens best when it informs the work of many people and organizations. One teacher improving instruction is good, one school is better, and a whole system is best. A strong orientation toward improvement does not mean that an organization welcomes failure. Taking risks does not guarantee success. And success is not the reward for risk taking; learning is (Heath & Heath, 2017). In schools where improvement is expected and achieved, reflective risk taking is prioritized and studied. Using the principles of improvement science, schools plan for improvement, implement changes, study those changes, and then act based on the evidence they collect. And they do this over and over in a never-ending cycle of improvement—ideally, in networks of schools to learn quickly even when they know what they are doing is probably incomplete (Bryk et al., 2015). This process of reflection, risk, and revision or rejection is informed by a professional learning network focused on thoughtful attempts at improvement (Eckert, 2016). In Chapter 7, we explore how collective leadership cultivates this strong orientation toward improvement.

Work Design

How do we think differently about the way we design the structures that support the work of teachers and administrators? Unfortunately, in the United States many people believe that teachers are only working when they are with students. Additionally, many administrators no longer teach students. In other countries, teaching is a profession where planning, co-teaching, assessment, and redesigning lessons are valued parts of the workday. Administrators are "head teachers" and maintain a presence in classrooms, either teaching their own classes or teaching alongside others. Chapter 8 will examine how to change the way we think about the work of teachers and administrators and the evolution of education.

Looking Ahead

In the subsequent chapters, as we address each of these seven conditions and associated practices, it's important to keep in mind that they are all interrelated conditions. As you diagnose your school or district, remember that four conditions (shared vision and strategy, supportive administration, resources and capacity, and work design) are antecedents to the remaining three (supportive social norms and working relationships, shared influence, and orientation toward improvement), but all of them overlap and influence the others. If you start working on a problem of practice by addressing one condition and find that you are not making progress, start working from a different condition.

The Collective Leadership Conditions Matrix (see Figure 1.3) is designed to help school leaders analyze what conditions might be lacking in their school based on the results they are getting. (These results are described as feelings shared across a team or staff because these tend to be nearly universal responses to underlying issues, which can snowball into additional cultural concerns.) To use the tool, look at the "Results" column. Which word or phrase best describes your school? Once you have identified the word or phrase, look at the columns to the left to see what might be missing. Compare your response with those of your colleagues. Do you agree or disagree with them? This exercise can be a great starter for a conversation about how different people view your school.

FIGURE 1.3

A Matrix for Understanding Team Challenges

MIRA EDUCATION — COLLECTIVE LEADERSHIP CONDITIONS MATRIX

	Vision & Strategy	Supportive Administration	Capacity & Resources	Work Structures	Relationships & Social Norms	Shared Influence	Orientation to Improve	RESULTS
	●	●	●	●	●	●	●	IMPACT
		●	●	●	●	●	●	CONFUSION
	●		●	●		●	●	INACTION
	●	●		●		●	●	FRUSTRATION
	●		●		●	●	●	LACK OF SUSTAINABILITY
	●	●	●	●		●	●	FRICTION
	●	●	●	●			●	BURNOUT
	●	●	●	●	●	●		NO CHANGE

If you come to a consensus on where your school needs to grow and are pressed for time, feel free to skip to the chapter associated with the relevant condition. We think all of the chapters matter and that there is something to be learned from the examples in each of them, but we know how limited time can be!

With those time constraints in mind, we've done some things a little differently in this book. Every chapter contains research and big-picture thinking to help shape your understanding of shifts in practice that move you and your team toward effective collective leadership. Each offers at least one related story from a school or district with which we've worked, so you can see how those shifts work in real, imperfect places with educators who share your struggles and successes. Then we turn to tools, similar to those used by leadership teams, that can help you apply ideas to your own and your team's leadership practice. And in place of a traditional conclusion, we close each chapter with a "wayfinding summary" meant to guide you to related sections of the book that might help you decide where to look next—so you can spend less time reading about shifts and more time practicing them.

2

Adapting, Not Adopting: Creating a Shared Vision and Strategy for Change

A principal with whom we worked faced a daunting task: consolidating two very different schools into one. Among other variables, one of those schools was facing state sanctions. Understandably, the staff at each school were concerned about their students, themselves, and what would become of "their" school. People had questions such as "Why should we have to live with sanctions imposed on the other school?" and "How will we ensure that our primary students are safe and nurtured when there are students up to 10 years older than them?" Challenges with culture and progress were evident.

The fastest path for the principal to create the new school's vision and mission may have been to close herself in her office and create *her* vision for the school. In fact, it is not at all unusual for designated leaders to feel pressure to do this and to then work with staff to create buy-in. However, when faced with the challenging situation of consolidating two schools, this leader chose a different path. She understood the need for all staff members to come together and cocreate a shared vision for their school and the strategy for how they were going to get there. She knew that if the vision and strategy were cocreated, then everyone would own the work to make that vision a reality and lean into it during challenging times. Her belief in cocreation led her to develop a process and structure that invited all staff to the vision and strategy cocreation "table."

The process that the team used was simple in its structure but powerful in how it created ownership and responsibility for outcomes. This principal strategically created diverse teams of staff members so that everyone had a chance to get to know one another and gain firsthand knowledge about the needs and concerns of colleagues. These teams were not limited to instructional staff. Rather, they were made up of certified and noncertified staff and other support professionals from the building. Again, the principal understood that engaging all staff in the creation of a vision was essential to generating shared ownership of the work ahead.

As the pandemic hit, the team was seven months into the implementation of a cocreated vision that had resulted in the development of strong relationships and social norms (see Chapter 5 for more on supportive social norms and working relationships). Though their strategies had to shift because of the sudden move to online and hybrid learning, their common understanding of where they were headed allowed them to be resilient in the face of crisis. Their resilience was grounded in their ability to work with and lead one another. In the midst of a pandemic that decimated educator efficacy nationwide, this school observed the *opposite* trend. In a survey of this and other schools practicing collective leadership in 2021, more than 67 percent of the teachers (compared to 45 percent in 2018) described themselves as leaders in the building, and 831 out of 886 (94 percent) "agreed" or "strongly agreed" that they worked well with other educators to accomplish that vision.

Collective leadership involves working toward shared goals that are aligned to a shared vision. Resilience in the face of change relies on co-ownership of a shared vision, which can then be used to create a cohesive approach for school improvement. Leadership can certainly occur in a school without a shared vision and strategies, but if 30 different teachers and administrators are "leading" without any followers or coherence across initiatives, the school will make little organizational progress.

Challenges and Shifts

As illustrated by the story that opened this chapter, shared vision and the strategies for how to attain that vision should not be created by one leader with the expectation that others will buy into it. Rather, shared vision should be developed through the collective expertise of school leaders: teachers and

FIGURE 2.1
Leadership Shifts for Shared Vision and Strategy

Moving from . . .	Shifting to . . .
Siloed decision making	Facilitating inclusive cocreation of the vision and strategy
Static vision statements	Contextualizing the vision according to evolving needs
Inflexible action plans	Crafting a strategy that is responsive to lessons learned

administrators (Bryk et al., 2010; Leithwood & Louis, 2012; Light, 1998). Shared vision and strategies drive instructional improvement and are the foundation for continuous school improvement (Fullan, 2005; Hargreaves & Fink, 2006; McCauley, 2008; Mumford et al., 2007; Smylie, 2010). The collective expertise that drives the shared vision is best developed by creating opportunities for teachers and administrators to work together.

In our work with schools and districts, we have seen three shifts that set the stage for the cocreation of a vision and strategy for collective leadership that result in resilience and sustainable change (see Figure 2.1).

Siloed Decision Making → Facilitating Inclusive Cocreation of the Vision and Strategy

Often school leaders are told that, to be strong leaders, they need to create or articulate their vision, set the strategy for how to realize that vision, work to build buy-in, and then hold staff accountable to the vision and strategy. This approach not only does not work but also does not result in sustainable change or resilience in the face of challenge. This failure occurs because it is difficult for people to know how to adjust when challenges arise if they were not actively engaged in creating the vision for where the organization is going or the strategies for how to get there. (See Chapter 3 for more about the impact of seeking buy-in rather than ownership.)

Perhaps the biggest challenge associated with one person crafting the vision and strategy is the potential for bias to be embedded in the result. Everyone holds biases based on their unique cultural conditioning and life experiences (Cherry, 2020), and these biases affect our understanding, actions, and decisions in an unconscious manner (Staats et al., 2015). Including people with diverse perspectives and roles in the cocreation of the vision and strategy is more likely to result in something that is less subject to bias and is more equitable.

Cocreation of the vision and strategy makes both of them resilient to change because everyone is "in the room" when agreements are made about where the team is headed and how they are going to get there. Once that information is known, challenges along the way can be met by the creation of alternative pathways that can ultimately get the team to the intended destination.

Static Vision Statements → Contextualizing the Vision According to Evolving Needs

It is likely that your school or district already has a vision statement in place. It is also likely that the vision statement cannot be changed without significant amounts of time, effort, and energy, none of which is in abundant supply, even if there is the will to do so.

That said, schools *are* likely to have a significant amount of flexibility in designing the strategy for achieving the stated vision. What your team *can* likely do is collectively craft a vision that expresses what the larger, static vision means for *your* school or district at *this* time and for *these* learners, as well as the strategies for how to realize that vision. For example, part of the vision statement for one of the schools with which we work includes the following language: "provides *engaging educational opportunities* through . . . *involvement in our diverse community.*" Although the vision statement itself is not likely to be altered, there is a range of possibilities for what "engaging educational opportunities" and "involvement in our diverse community" might mean at *this* time, for *these* learners. This is where cocreation of a vision and strategy can take place without tackling the larger task of rewriting the school's overall vision statement. Once agreements are made for what the vision means for the people in *this* school or district at *this* time, they can be used as touchstones for decision making and how to proceed regardless of the situation, thus increasing resilience.

For instance, in the example just offered, once the team has defined what is meant by "engaging educational opportunities" and "involvement in our diverse community," they can begin to ask themselves questions such as these: *In what ways does this [lesson, event, strategy, professional learning, and so on] align with our definition of "engaging educational opportunity"? How does this support "engagement in our diverse community"?* If the answers to those questions are that it does not, they can decide not to do it or to redesign whatever is being implemented to align with the vision.

Inflexible Action Plans → Crafting a Strategy That Is Responsive to Lessons Learned

Schools are frequently required to develop action plans that outline the goals and strategies on which they will focus for the year and the metrics they will use to measure progress against those stated goals. This requirement is particularly prevalent in schools that are labeled as "underperforming." Although it is helpful to have a sense of what your team is intending to accomplish and how you plan to get there, plans that are rigid and do not allow for midcourse corrections may not be as helpful as they could be.

We suggest a shift to the development of a strategy that allows for the articulation of successes, challenges, and lessons learned and the use of that information to make midcourse corrections. Building structures for identifying and using information about what is working, what is not, and what your team is learning along the way will help create a strategy that is adaptive to current conditions and create a space for innovation, which is discussed further in Chapter 7.

Creating a Vision in Times of Crisis: A District in Illinois

In early 2020, the vision statement of a school district in Illinois was to create equitable, inclusive learning environments for all students in order to offer a positive educational experience for the whole child. That spring, when the pandemic hit, the district's collective commitment to that vision was tested, and its response demonstrated its willingness and capacity to embody the vision.

Before we delve into the actions the district took in response to the pandemic, let's take a moment to understand its commitment to equity, which played a central role in how it responded to this crisis. During the three years before March 2020, the district actively engaged a wide range of stakeholders in the development of an equity policy that reinforces an ongoing community commitment to equity, racial and social justice, and belonging for all learners within the district, with the goal of providing equitable access to a public education that meets their needs and prepares them for college and career. In addition to having a robust equity policy, the district has also embedded inclusion and antiracism into its teaching and learning department, signaling the importance of integrating equity across their teaching and learning system.

As the 2019–20 school year started, the district began to fully implement its equity policy. Then in March 2020, the pandemic hit, shutting down schools across the United States. Because of the groundwork that had been laid related to the district's commitment to and vision of an equitable and inclusive learning environment, it quickly took action to prepare its educators to meet the needs of their students—especially those with the fewest opportunities to do well under the circumstances.

The district understood that how well students would learn that year had everything to do with how its teachers were supported to make the shift to online and hybrid learning. The team also understood that even if districts were able to bring students back for some in-person learning in fall 2020, the outlook for how *educators* would be supported was less clear. The district wasn't leaving its goals for equity and effectiveness to chance. Its leaders needed to be sure that teachers could still access continuous, high-quality coaching and professional learning. We partnered with the district to help ensure that teachers could do just that, and we supported their transition to virtual professional learning.

District leaders developed a strategy to build capacity for sustaining virtual learning communities and support on three levels. Coaches needed to offer effective, engaging online professional learning for current educators and new hires. Principals needed to build community and efficacy among staff, parents, and students in challenging times. Other educators needed quick access to essentials for building equitable classroom cultures, even when classrooms weren't physical spaces.

To accomplish these goals, district leaders cleared agendas for coaches' and administrators' regular meetings over one-month periods. This freed time and space to engage in Mira Education's Cultivating Communities for Impact (CCI) experience. Each cohort had opportunities to learn best practices for building rapport, engagement, and effective learning. Facilitators coached participants to design and practice actual sessions they'd lead later in the summer. An extra professional development day at the close of the school year was repurposed for all instructional staff to join targeted, 90-minute, online workshops to prepare them for teaching in the fall.

As a result of this work, coaches and administrators were prepared as facilitators of online professional learning and support for instructional staff; hundreds of teachers had a starting-skills toolkit for online teaching and learning for the fall of 2020; and nearly all participants strongly agreed that CCI was relevant to the work ahead of them.

The ability of these educators to respond quickly, manage the crisis, and be resilient while doing so was grounded in their collective vision and commitment to equity. Because everyone understood where they were headed and who they intended to be during the crisis, they were able to respond in ways that aligned with their vision to better serve all the learners within their system.

Strategies to Support the Shifts

Before working through strategies and using the tools for engaging in the shifts outlined earlier in this chapter, you may want to assess how your team is doing with cocreating a shared vision and strategy by using the self-assessment that is available as part of the Collective Leadership Playbook (Mira Education, n.d.). Completing the self-assessment (Figure 2.2) can provide insight into how your team may wish to proceed in using the strategies and tools shared here.

FIGURE 2.2

A Tool to Facilitate the Cocreation of a Vision

Teams: How will we create diverse teams? Age? Grade/content? Experience? Ability? Race/ethnicity? Role? What else?

Team 1				
Team 2				
Team 3				
Team 4				
Team 5				
Team 6				
Team 7				

When the vision for _____ [department, school, district] is realized, what will we or our learners think, see, say, feel, hear? (Write your responses in the spaces below.)

Think	See	Say	Feel	Hear

Know: What should learners *know* as a result of their engagement with our class/school/department?	**Do:** What should learners *do* as a result of their engagement with our class/school/department?

Notes and keywords to include in our vision statement.

What verb applies to the vision your team intends to create?

Who is your clientele?

What three adjectives speak to the values related to this work?

What is the ultimate goal you are intending to achieve?

Strategy 1: Construct Diverse Teams

As your team engages in your own process for cocreating a shared vision for a collectively led effort, we suggest you start by strategically dividing staff members into diverse teams based on the range of roles and responsibilities that are represented across the group. Doing so will allow members of each team to connect directly with colleagues who have different perspectives and responsibilities. These diverse teams will also create opportunities for participants to gather firsthand information about the lived experiences of colleagues. This empathy data will help to inform the work of cocreating the vision and strategy and is likely to strengthen professional relationships among staff members. (See Chapter 5 for more on this topic.)

While constructing teams, also consider intentionally and strategically engaging those who have been historically underrepresented or those with diverse perspectives. The tool in Figure 2.3 can support your efforts to identify and connect with a range of stakeholders and invite them into collective leadership conversations and decision making. Strategic efforts to elevate and integrate underrepresented perspectives and experiences will support efforts to build a more equitable and inclusive environment. Questions for discussion as you use this tool include the following:

- Column 1: Who is historically underrepresented in decision making at this school/district? What perspectives are missing?
- Column 2: What in our practice might explain why the people/ perspectives in Column 1 are underrepresented? What factors within our control are in play that may inhibit participation or contribution?
- Column 3: What might we do to connect with those who are usually underrepresented? How might we address inhibiting factors?
- Column 4: What is our best next step to connect with underrepresented groups and to address inhibiting factors that limit their engagement?

Strategy 2: Reach Consensus on "Know" and "Do"

Once teams have been established, they should discuss and come to some consensus on what learners and leaders in the school or district should know and be able to do as a result of engagement with the community. Teams should

FIGURE 2.3

A Tool for Building Diverse Teams

From whom do we need to hear?	What in our practice might explain why we have not engaged diverse perspectives?	What might we do to engage those who are historically underrepresented?	What is our best next step, who will take it, and by when?

consider the knowledge, skills, and dispositions that characterize someone who is actively engaged in collective leadership within the school or district. Questions for discussion could include the following:

- **Know.** What would successful collective leaders know how to do when interacting with one another to make decisions? What skills would successful collective leaders possess, and how might they go about developing those skills?

- **Do.** What would collective leaders be able to do that would allow them to be successful when engaging with colleagues? What evidence would we see to know that they were being successful leaders?

Defining what successful leaders know and can do will provide a "north star" for people to look to when they are faced with challenges or are unsure about how to proceed. Articulating the elements of success allows the vision to be resilient and provides clarity around where everyone is trying to go while also providing flexibility to choose different paths for how to get there.

Strategy 3: Contextualize the Vision

It is likely that your school or district already has a vision statement that your team may not have the ability or opportunity to change. If so, it is equally likely that your team has some degree of flexibility in how that vision statement can be defined and the strategies that you can choose to implement it. This is where contextualizing the vision comes into play. Your team can leverage any available flexibility to define success for each component of your vision statement. The tool in Figure 2.4 can be used to do exactly that: contextualize your current vision statement to define success—what it looks, feels, and sounds like—for *these* learners at *this* time.

Start by entering the current vision statement at the top of the tool. Then, as a team, identify the different components of your school's vision statement. (If the vision statement you are working with has more than three components, simply use multiple copies of the tool.) As an example, one of the schools mentioned earlier in the chapter has the following vision

FIGURE 2.4
A Tool for Contextualizing the Vision

Current vision statement:	
Vision Components	**Defining This Context**
Key component 1	What does successful realization of this component look like for these learners at this time?
Key component 2	What does successful realization of this component look like for these learners at this time?
Key component 3	What does successful realization of this component look like for these learners at this time?

statement: "Anonymous High School provides *engaging educational opportunities* through a *rigorous curriculum, innovative technology,* and *involvement in our diverse community* to produce *responsible citizens* who *contribute to the present* and *excel in the future*." In this case, the team might identify the different components as the following:

- Engaging educational opportunities
- Rigorous curriculum
- Innovative technology
- Involvement in our diverse community
- Responsible citizens
- Contribute to the present
- Excel in the future

Your team may choose to divide key topics in the vision statement differently. Whatever your team decides, the key components should be entered into the boxes on the left side of the tool.

In the second column, have your team enter information about what successful implementation or realization of that component would look like for *these* learners at *this* time. For instance, when your team says "engaging educational opportunities," what does that mean? How does your team define that phrase? What components would be present, and what would learners be doing if an educational opportunity were engaging? As your team addresses these questions, seek to create consensus around how your team will define "engaging educational opportunities" and enter it into the appropriate box. Continue working through the different components of the vision statement until you have defined success or the criteria your team will use to determine whether or not something is aligned to your contextualized vision statement.

Once you have contextualized the vision statement, your team can use that information for decision making. Experiences, activities, strategies, or approaches that are being considered for implementation can be tested against the contextualized version of the vision statement to determine whether or not to proceed. Establishing and practicing this process will allow for resilience in the face of crisis because everyone will be using the same definition and criteria for decision making.

Wayfinding Summary

Cocreating a vision and strategy for collective leadership may take more time, effort, and energy than would be required if only one individual were undertaking the task. However, it is worth the up-front investment to ensure your team has a shared understanding of where improvement efforts are aimed and how you will get there. Without that understanding, you will find yourself caught up in frequent questions or missteps based on differing assumptions, or you will see that efforts are unsuccessful or unsustainable without your direct involvement. Untangling these issues usually takes even more time than building up a shared understanding at the outset.

The process of building shared vision and strategy is complex. If you find yourself getting bogged down, you can visit the chapters specified in the following list to get ideas about other conditions that may be affecting your team so that you can unlock progress:

- Co-ownership results from the development of a shared vision and strategy, and it takes supportive administration (Chapter 3) to ensure that action is possible.
- Relationships and social norms (Chapter 5) allow for effective communication that will ensure effective cocreation and, therefore, co-ownership of the shared vision and strategy.
- At the end of the day, work designs that are sustainable and responsive to changing needs are ones that ensure your team's efforts toward the vision are aligned, not ad hoc (Chapter 8).

3

Co-Ownership, Not Buy-In: Engaging Collective Expertise Through Supportive Administration

A district was simultaneously implementing new systems for teacher and administrator evaluation, a new compensation structure, and a new curriculum in different subject areas at all grade levels. Most school administrators had not been consulted on these changes but were expected to buy in on the initiatives and "push them down to teachers" whether they agreed with the changes or not. Teachers complained to school administrators that they felt these initiatives were "being done to them" instead of "being developed with them"—a key strategy for developing shared vision that we discussed in Chapter 2. School administrators were expected to support the district policies and ensure that they were implemented with fidelity.

This story is not unique. We have seen it repeatedly and could insert one of countless names for the district. This approach might take more time or add to the complexity of initial planning and decision making as it engages the expertise within a community and defines leadership as work toward shared goals. It requires a wide range of people to step into leadership. Instead of one person getting buy-in from others, the people doing the actual leadership work at the point of contact with students are bringing their experiences and hard-won wisdom to decision making. Administrators need both the confidence and the humility to support diverse opinions that might deviate from their own in order to get to solutions that will better serve their communities. As we move toward the collective expertise of a team, we move toward more diverse, equitable, and inclusive leadership.

For the last three decades, we have seen empirical evidence that teachers are the most significant school-level influence on student learning (Hanushek, 1992; Rivkin et al., 2005; Sanders & Rivers, 1996). We also know that teaching has become increasingly challenging, with a loss of 567,000 public school educators between 2020 and 2022 and many teachers seeking additional support and autonomy (Dill, 2022; Gecker, 2021; Jotkoff, 2022; Kamenetz, 2022).

Although supporting high-quality teaching and learning is an adaptive challenge without easy answers, we know that supportive administration is an essential element in recruiting and especially retaining effective educators. School administrators have significant influence on student learning as well (DeMatthews et al., 2020; Lee et al., 2021; Louis et al., 2010; Waters et al., 2003). Lack of support from administration is one of the primary reasons why teachers leave their schools and the profession (Carver-Thomas & Darling-Hammond, 2017). Conversely, effective administrators can build cultures of collective teacher efficacy that cultivate competence and commensurate autonomy. As the term implies, "collective teacher efficacy" is efficacy that is co-owned. Through their work with visible learning, Australian researcher John Hattie and his team have found that collective teacher efficacy—educators' belief that they can effectively influence student learning—is the single most influential factor on student learning (Hattie, 2018). For the last five years, we have been tracking the collective efficacy of teachers and administrators in South Carolina, with more than 7,000 survey responses. Schools in which supportive administration is highly rated by teachers typically have a higher level of collective efficacy (see Figure 3.1).

Supporting the survey results, a 2010 study found that collective leadership was significantly more effective than more traditional approaches (Louis et al., 2010). If collective leadership is going to affect student outcomes, then administrators will have to support the good work of others and acknowledge that they lead more effectively when they share power, elevate others' voices, and consider themselves as storytellers and supporters.

FIGURE 3.1

Collective Leadership Survey Scores Compared to Collective Teacher Efficacy Scores

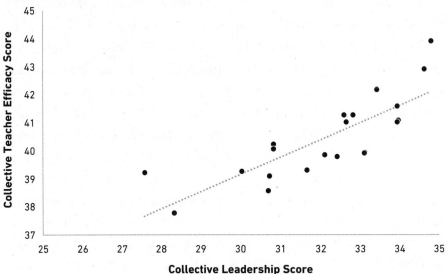

Supportive administration also can provide increased autonomy through collective leadership. People in all sectors thrive when they gain autonomy that is commensurate with their enhanced competence (Deci & Flaste, 1995). At a time when collective expertise is needed more than ever, we must allow educators to flourish by providing avenues for leadership that build on their expertise. However, to build on the collective expertise of our schools and districts, we do *not* need to get people to "buy in."

What do we think of when we hear the phrase "buy-in"? It sounds like someone with some positional authority is using the power dynamic to manipulate, sell, or convince subordinates to adopt a solution that is not their own. That is why technical solutions proliferate and do little to address rampant adaptive challenges. In fact, top-down solutions that do not consider the experiences of those leading the work that we are trying to improve have little opportunity to be anything but technical.

If you are a leader who is on the treadmill of trying to get buy-in, now is the time to jump off. Attempting to get buy-in is exhausting and rarely gets us where we want to go. Adaptive solutions require deep knowledge of the underlying challenges and their nuances. For example, asking school administrators and teachers to "buy in" to a regimen of standardized testing and accountability handed down from state officials without understanding the teaching and learning conditions in classrooms will breed cynicism. Conversely, engaging school administrators and teachers in conversations about how to use a range of data to better understand teaching and learning in a range of contexts gets a school closer to an adaptive improvement.

Administrators who lead through co-ownership are less concerned about who gets credit for improvement and are more focused on the improvement itself. Supportive administrators are sometimes referred to as being "multipliers" (Wiseman, 2017) or "catalysts." As in chemistry, where a catalyst accelerates a reaction without being used up itself, a leader who is a catalyst accelerates adaptive change. No matter what we call them, administrators create the threshold condition for all other leadership work by developing solutions that are co-owned. Co-owned solutions are superior for at least five reasons:

- They are more likely to be implemented.
- Those doing the work are more likely to follow through on the work.
- They are more sustainable because they are not dependent on any one person.
- They are more likely to make us aware of our biases and reduce bias in our decision making.
- They are more likely to work.

Being a supportive administrator is not about being well-liked or magnanimous. Supportive administrators who are catalysts lead pragmatically. They know that they are coaches who are helping to set a coherent vision and working with team members to increase the likelihood of success. In doing so, they preserve themselves, elevate the good work of others, and can celebrate success that is not just their own but is shared. As noted earlier, catalysts are multipliers (Wiseman, 2017). Multipliers assume that they work with talented people who can figure out problems on their own in order to accelerate good work in sustainable ways.

In this chapter, we will explore concrete ways to become catalytic leaders who are multipliers. We know that leadership flourishes in environments where leaders celebrate the success of others. How often do we do that as educators? Probably not often enough. However, we can move from being educators who are diminishing to those who are thriving if we can make the following three shifts: (1) from *the* leader to leadership, (2) from commander-in-chief to storytelling, and (3) from position to work.

Challenges and Shifts

The shifts described here, and shown in Figure 3.2, primarily focus on how to change the way we view leadership from identity, or role, to action. For example, "leader" is a role; "leadership" is an action.

The Leader → Leadership

Almost all school administrators will acknowledge that they cannot lead alone, yet many operate as if they do. The hard-charging principal or the teacher who is at work longer than everyone else and answers emails at all hours of the night still has a romanticized place in our collective mythology of leadership (think of movies such as *Lean on Me, Stand and Deliver, Freedom Writers*).

Some of this mythology is based on the way the system is structured (see more in Chapter 8), as well as the way leaders themselves structure organizations. For example, as we noted earlier, male leaders are more likely to set up hierarchies, whereas women are more likely to create webs of interconnected leaders with themselves in the middle (Bolman & Deal, 2017).

FIGURE 3.2

Leadership Shifts for Supportive Administration

Moving from . . .	Shifting to . . .
The leader	Leadership
Commander-in-chief	Storytelling
Position	Work

A lack of hierarchy and an interconnectedness of coleaders are more likely to support catalytic improvement. The following questions offer a couple of ways to tell if we are more likely serving as a catalyst or *the* leader.

- How is the school's leadership structured? Is it more of a hierarchy or a web? If it is more of a hierarchy, how can we move toward a web?
- What was the last idea that someone else had that we worked to accelerate? If we find that we are always trying to get buy-in for our own ideas, maybe we are not yet the catalysts we hope to be.

If we can make this shift from being *the* leader (a position or role) to leadership (an action), we can avoid some common leadership pitfalls. Trying to assume the role of the lone leader as opposed to a supportive leader of leaders causes us to feel overwhelmed and overworked, and it limits our ability to lead adaptive improvement because of the limits of our knowledge. Given the complexity and challenges our schools currently face, co-ownership of improvement is more necessary than ever. In *Leading Together* (Eckert, 2018), through a series of case studies in urban, suburban, and rural schools, we asserted that the old maxim "many hands make light work" was actually not strong enough for what schools require. Instead, we argued that "many hands make the work possible." As leaders, when we get tired of being overwhelmed, overworked, or ignorant, the best remedy is to find others doing good work and do whatever we can to help accelerate that success.

Part of this shift is moving from leaders viewing themselves as *managers* of others to *supporters* of others. In general, people do not want to be managed; they want to be supported. This is true of people who become managers as well. They want support from their supervisors—support that helps them improve. The desire for improvement is hard-wired into human beings, and we respond well to feedback and support when we believe they lead to our flourishing. We are much less receptive to judgment and evaluation (Bleiberg et al., 2021). Every organization needs leaders and managers, but, as noted, few of us really want to be managed. The literature makes a distinct difference between a leader and a manager. Simply put, leaders do the right thing, and managers do things right (Bolman & Deal, 2017). In schools, the manager might be doing things right in ways that support district administration even when the action might be wrong for students.

What if management felt more like support? The challenge of this manifestation of leadership is that it takes a confidently humble (Grant, 2021) leader who is willing to share decision-making power. The required confident humility flows from an understanding that an individual leader cannot have all of the answers and is therefore a conduit to better ideas by supporting the spread of expertise in a given organization. The ultimate indicator that principals have moved from serving as commanders-in-chief and managers to catalytic supporters is how they share decision making, particularly related to instructional leadership. How do principals help leaders in the school determine what is best for their students? In healthy schools, the principal is the "lead learner," not the "commander-in-chief." (See Chapter 5 for more on how to operate as a lead learner.)

Commander-in-Chief → Storytelling

Why do we use military terminology when discussing schools? The military provides an extreme example of hierarchical leadership. A clear chain of command connects the commander-in-chief to the lowliest private. When going to war, this hierarchy is essential to reduce confusion, order soldiers into battle, and work efficiently toward objectives identified by commanding officers. We talk about teachers being "in the trenches" or "on the front lines," but we are not going to war. In fact, we are doing just the opposite. We are attempting to engage the hearts and minds of each student in ways that see and know each one as a whole human being. We do not want to reduce thinking, compromise improvement for efficiency, or have to make decisions about who will live or die. Command-and-control structures are needed when following orders and "not thinking" are required. Most schools and districts have structures and policies in place that leaders can initiate when circumstances require them, such as lockdown drills and health and safety protocols. However, schools are primarily about thinking and problem solving and are, therefore, not ideally led by commanders-in-chief.

What if administrators embraced their roles not as generals seeking the buy-in of soldiers to a mission, but as communicators? *What if principals transitioned from telling people what to do to telling people what others are doing?* One principal of a comprehensive high school has embraced this role. He describes himself as the "storyteller-in-chief." He believes his primary role is to support and highlight the good work of teachers and students. To do this, his school requires waivers for pictures and videos from every student. As he conducts walkthroughs, he takes pictures and records brief learning experiences. As soon as he leaves the room, he posts the pictures and videos to social media to "make the walls of the school glass" (Eckert & Butler, 2021). This kind of leadership does at least three things:

- **The storyteller-in-chief elevates the work in classrooms and makes everyday successes public.** Other teachers see the posts, as do parents and community members, which creates an environment that celebrates the success of others.
- **The culture changes.** Sharing victories in the classroom cultivates a supportive atmosphere, publicly celebrating work that would typically go unnoticed behind closed classroom doors.
- **Additional resources become available.** One of the principal's primary purposes is to bring in additional resources. Through multiple partnerships with community organizations and industries, his school benefits when the partners see their investments paying off in the form of engaged learning.

Practices like this can build a culture of inclusive celebration of individual successes. In talking to teachers in this building, they regularly highlight and praise the work of their colleagues. Having many people celebrate the work of others minimizes the likelihood of bias in terms of which stories might be told and reduces the risk that only particular individuals or successes might be highlighted.

Position → Work

Supportive administrators do not see leadership as a position or a set of character traits. Instead, leadership is about work toward shared goals. (Chapter 6 explores how to cocreate those goals.) Surveys and focus groups show that schools are more likely to be engaged in collective leadership when teachers and administrators believe that leadership is more about the *work* than the *person* (Eckert, 2018). We know leadership is dependent on both the person and the work, so why does it matter if educators believe that it is more about the work? Our theory is that people are more likely to step into leadership work if they do not believe that they need a particular position or certain leadership characteristics to do it. If, instead, they believe that they are *able* to do the work and have the power and autonomy to lead the work, they do so.

Principals and assistant principals who do not lean on their titles for power tacitly communicate to their teams that leadership is not directly correlated with position. Principals and assistant principals who communicate that leadership is not about charisma and extroversion but about influencing others to do better work are more likely to develop other leaders and, more important, improve student outcomes (Eckert, 2018; Eckert & Butler, 2021).

Additionally, research in schools finds that leaders who operate as bridge-builders and connectors are significantly more likely to be leading effective schools (Bryk et al., 2010; Bryk & Schneider, 2002; DiPaola & Tschannen-Moran, 2005). The role of a school principal is often to bridge while buffering—connecting leaders who are doing meaningful work where there is mutual benefit while keeping external bureaucratic requirements to a minimum. We all appreciate leaders who connect us to others who help us improve while at the same time eliminating distracting paperwork. When teachers can focus on their instructional work, students and teachers are more likely to flourish.

Explicating the Challenges and Shifts

We need to be clear about the overarching shift of this chapter. By shifting from buy-in to co-ownership, we are not supporting death by committee, analysis paralysis, or additional meaningless bureaucratic red tape. Jon can provide an illustrative example of what we do not mean: the Committee on Committees. When he first arrived at Baylor University, a colleague mentioned this group, and Jon thought it was some type of joke. He found out, however, that Baylor does actually have a committee with this name whose purpose is to create committees.

Some concepts found in the leadership literature—*distribute, delegate, anoint, appoint,* and *manage*—do not necessarily support co-owning leadership. Here is why:

- *Distribute* can connote a central leadership figure who is determining who should have power from a limited and exclusive "pool" of power.

- *Delegate* communicates a similar notion of central planning that determines, by fiat, who should do what work. Although delegation is a necessary skill for any leader, the term can be a barrier to co-ownership, particularly when we seek more diverse voices in leadership processes.

- *"Anoint and appoint"* approaches to leadership have been pervasive in school districts for decades (Smylie & Denny, 1990). In these cases, one person serves as the kingmaker for leaders within a school or district by dictating who will be elevated into leadership positions. This method is particularly problematic for getting out of the leadership echo chamber, where the same voices lead to the same solutions, because often we are drawn to others who think in similar ways to ourselves.

- *Manage* is an important word, but it can be misused. As we noted earlier, *leadership* and *management* are not synonymous. Co-ownership of leadership will require effective management of processes, but many administrators will need to fight the urge to manage—or worse, micromanage—all aspects of the work that flows through the process.

Because some of these terms and approaches to leadership are so pervasive, co-ownership is not the norm. If co-ownership is to become the norm, administrators will need to understand their bias toward the status quo. When confronted with change, many of us will see change only as risk and the status quo as what is safe. However, the status quo involves risk as well, and we have to help administrators see this reality. In 10 years, schools will be different because the students and communities we serve will be different. A school that does not adapt faces a significant risk that its students will not thrive. Through co-ownership of leadership—leadership that is catalyzed by supportive administrators—schools are more likely to adapt to the needs of their community while maintaining a shared vision for education because the people doing the school's core work are influencing its direction.

However, co-ownership is not suitable for every situation. Certain administrative tasks (e.g., bus routes, facilities, certain aspects of budgeting) do not require the collective expertise of teachers and administrators. Administrators might have particular skills and knowledge that make them the right person to manage many facilities issues and other administrative tasks. Certainly, there are times when it is appropriate to bring teachers together to discuss the best use of facilities or to make scheduling decisions, but co-owning leadership does not mean that everyone should have a say in every decision, which would be undesirable for all involved.

Instruction is the primary area that requires the collective leadership and development of teachers and administrators. We need to continue to move away from the notion of the principal as *the* instructional leader toward the notion of the principal leaning upon the instructional expertise of teachers who are at the point of contact with students. In fact, administrators who remove bureaucratic red tape and unnecessary administrative tasks from teachers create more time for meaningful co-owned leadership. For example, instead of using staff meetings to review administrative procedures and district-driven policies, this information can be conveyed via email or newsletter, creating time during staff meetings to share what is working well instructionally, which allows for more deliberation that teachers and administrators can co-lead.

Co-ownership is messy, we admit. Whenever we cease functioning like benevolent dictators and solicit the views of others, we add to the complexity of our thinking. However, in the long run, if we get to better solutions, the messiness is more than worth the time and energy. For example, when discussing how to implement a Multi-Tiered System of Supports (MTSS) designed to meet the needs of each student, a single administrator describing how this should be done and delegating responsibility to various individuals is an ignorantly efficient way to implement. An approach grounded in ignorance will likely founder and is, therefore, not actually efficient. People might appear to go along with MTSS for a while, but if they do not own the process, the needs of each student will not be met. Engaging all members of a school community who have expertise in and responsibility for implementing MTSS at the front end of the process will increase the likelihood of success in the long run.

Let's turn to what it looks like for administrators or others in formal leadership positions to promote a team's engagement and co-ownership of work, starting with a case study of a partner district.

Improving Leadership with Teacher Leaders: School District of Philadelphia

The School District of Philadelphia invested in teacher leadership early and literally. Starting in 2006, the district allotted extra funds to *every* school serving grades K–8 to create positions for school-based teacher leaders (SBTLs). The model did maximize flexibility at the school level, allowing principals to design the roles and processes that they thought worked best for their buildings. However, flexibility came at a cost. Eleven years later, the central office had little idea about how SBTLs supported other educators and students, how well they scaled up strong instructional practice, or even who occupied the roles.

The district might have resolved the challenge by taking back control for hiring and supporting the positions. Instead, the Office of Teaching and Learning (OTL) decided the best approach wasn't to centralize decisions but to make them more transparent. Mira Education had the opportunity to work with OTL on a three-part process: (1) conducting a scan of SBTL positions to establish a common understanding of best practices; (2) convening a design team (including SBTLs, principals, district office staff, and union representatives); and (3) facilitating their experimentation and thinking about new ways to build more such capacity without sacrificing flexibility.

Over seven months, the design team codeveloped several effective tools to support amplified success for SBTLs. These included models for effective co-teaching and "real-time coaching" between SBTLs and teachers, as well as refinement of position descriptions that incorporated learnings from schools across the district and made hiring easier for principals. Most important, OTL was able to create a set of leadership standards for SBTLs and other teacher leaders and then craft an aligned Teacher Leadership Academy designed to support current SBTLs and train their eventual successors from among effective, peer-respected classroom teachers.

Strategies to Support the Shifts

Administrators and other formally recognized leaders often take on three key responsibilities in times of change: identifying opportunities for innovation or improvement, communicating about the changes, and offering support and guidance along the way. The strategies that follow are recommended shifts in how you may already be approaching these three elements in your leadership practice.

Strategy 1: Invite Others into Our Work and Enter into Theirs

As we see in the Philadelphia case study, we have to invite others into our work. When we do so, we must also offer to be a catalyst for resolving a problem or leveraging an opportunity that is important to them. As leaders, sometimes it is better to come alongside someone else's problems of practice rather than always being the person driving what the work will be. By inviting others in and allowing ourselves to be invited in, we have the potential to see challenges from different vantage points in ways that will support a better solution. Certainly, the co-owned Teacher Leadership Academy in Philadelphia is more likely to lead to success than previous "solutions" that might have been done *to* educators rather than *with* them.

If administrators are initiating the invitation, they have to understand that there is a power differential involved, and therefore they must be very intentional about this being a true invitation. For example, first-year untenured teachers are unlikely to share their true opinions about the efficacy of an induction program with a supervisor who can make consequential career decisions for them through an evaluation process. If the administrator owns the induction program, then most beginning teachers are going to give it positive feedback. However, if the administrator asks beginning teachers to help improve induction for the following year and is legitimately open to feedback for improvement, the result can include increased leadership capacity, goodwill, and a better induction program.

Making the Invitation

The invitations to co-ownership of leadership might begin with administrators doing this as a way to foster culture, but in addition, teachers need to invite others into their classrooms to make their work public. In a school where co-ownership and trust are the norms, these invitations should be extended to both teachers and administrators. Here is a process that outlines how we make these invitations gradually, cascading from easy connections into more complex and challenging ones:

1. The purpose of inviting others into our instructional practice is not to create more opportunities for evaluation and judgment, but to cultivate trust and a culture of improvement, as well as a sense that we teach better collectively than we do individually. If a school does not already exhibit these qualities, we start small with a willing group of partners.

2. Depending on a school team's readiness, the shift might require starting with only positive feedback of what we see in others' classrooms.

3. After a semester of focusing on positive feedback, we need to invite others to give us critical feedback on an area that could be observed in a 10- to 12-minute walkthrough. Before the observation, the individuals being observed determine the area where they want feedback. For example, they might want feedback on how well they engage particular groups of students.

4. The observers can specifically track the progress of those groups and give feedback after the walkthrough either on a form or a sticky note, or with a quick debrief. Giving the feedback does not have to take a lot of time, but this is how we change school culture and improve instruction.

Ultimately, the teacher leadership initiative in Philadelphia was successful because of the way teachers improved outcomes as a result of the invitational nature of the work. Administrators invited teacher leaders into the work, and the teachers developed meaningful solutions that improved their ability to collaborate around goals that mattered to them and their students.

Strategy 2: Find Positive Stories and Share Them with Others

We all enjoy positive feedback; however, the best way to give it is to spread positive stories through a school's culture. As administrators, teachers, or just human beings, identifying positive things that others are doing is a healthy habit. Certainly we should share what we see as positive with the person who is doing the good work, but what we share might be even more influential if we share it with others.

This "positive venting" does the opposite of what venting typically does. Venting about other people typically reduces the morale of at least three people: the person doing the venting, the person being vented to, and the person being vented about. Although the person doing the venting might feel better afterward because another person has confirmed a negative opinion of someone else, this slight boost is based on negative feelings that seem justified. Positive venting boosts the morale of the person doing the sharing and the person listening, and if the positive sharing gets back to the person being praised, another boost is nearly guaranteed.

A Process for Positive Venting

1. Each week for the next month, find at least one story of something that an educator in your school or district did that supported at least one student's learning.

2. Share that story with someone other than the educator involved.

3. Better yet, identify how a team of educators contributed to that student's learning. Supportive educators can break the Hollywood

narrative of the single teacher or administrator fighting for kids against an unjust system by elevating the stories of teams of teachers doing work that improves students' lives. Every case study in this book is an example of how teams lead.

4. After you have shared the story with someone else, share it with the educator who supported the learning. We can certainly share that positive story with the educator(s) involved, but we change a culture by celebrating stories with the broader community, whether on social media, through passing conversations in the hall, or in more formal ways. This practice also leads to individuals and communities flourishing (Seligman, 2011).

5. At the end of the month, check how you feel about your team. Additionally, identify any changes in the collective efficacy of the educators on your team. What, if anything, is different?

Strategy 3: Ask, "How Are You Doing? What Do You Need?"

Leaders identify others' needs and figure out ways to meet them. We become supporters instead of managers by asking two simple questions: "How are you doing?" and "What do you need?" Sometimes these are the only two questions administrators need to ask of their teams. Over time, as administrators become trusted sources of support, they might not need to ask these questions directly; team members may learn to proactively articulate the answers unprompted. Regardless, these questions provide an important framework for ensuring a balance of management *and* support for the work and for the people doing it.

This approach has two caveats. First, we must be sure to have other people asking us these questions as well. Believing that we can meet each need of every person will lead to burnout. We are catalysts, not saviors. We have to determine where we can help and where we cannot. Second, and most important, we have to follow through by connecting others with the resources and people they need.

Traits of Multipliers

Liz Wiseman (2017) considers leaders who are diminishers to have a mindset that says, "People cannot figure it out without me." She characterizes them with the following terms: *empire builder, tyrant, know-it-all, decision maker*, and *micromanager*. In contrast, she considers leaders who are multipliers to have a mindset that says, "People are smart and will figure it out" and characterizes them with the terms *talent magnet, liberator, challenger, debate maker*, and *investor* (Wiseman, 2017). Consider the following questions and write your answers down as you reflect:

- Are you more of a diminisher or a multiplier?

- Where do you excel and where do you need to grow?

- If you are feeling bold, ask a couple of trusted colleagues to tell you where you are succeeding as a multiplier. Ask them to identify where you might be falling short.

- Identify three next steps that you can take next week to be more of a multiplier.

Wayfinding Summary

As educators move from buy-in to co-ownership, administrators who view their leadership as being about support, storytelling, and *what they do within their roles* rather than *who they are simply because of their roles* will catalyze the growth and engagement of others. Supportive administration interacts with other collective leadership conditions to grow effective, productive teams. The following related elements are discussed in the noted chapters:

- Focusing on orientation toward improvement (Chapter 7) is an important way administrators can shift to a supportive mode *and* build a sense of collective efficacy through dedication to collective learning and leadership.

- Building supportive norms and working relationships (Chapter 5) helps teachers and administrators create a sense of empathy and psychological safety as they encounter the risks of leadership work together.
- Teachers and administrators become stronger practitioners of collective leadership and continuous improvement when they share influence (Chapter 6) over one another's thinking and work.

4

Mindful Use, Not More: Aligning Resources and Capacity to Get Change Off the Ground

Do any of these comments sound familiar?

- "I agree. That approach would be really helpful. But we're already implementing three new programs this year, so it'll have to wait."
- "The pilot was really promising, but the grant ended, so we're not continuing the work."
- "I'd love for us to take that on, but we all have too much on our plates as it is."
- "It would be great to teach that, but we can't afford the curriculum, training, or materials."
- "We need to continue tutoring, but there's no way to do that virtually with our volunteers."
- "I know there's no one else to lead that, but I'm already leading three committees, facilitating the SIT, coordinating MTSS, and supporting PLCs with data. I can't do one more thing!"
- "It would be worth a try, but our district just doesn't have capacity to support that."

If you haven't said these things as a school leader, you've likely heard them from your team. Every "but" represents a promising idea that you and your staff may be setting aside because you feel constrained by resources: energy, attention, money, time, supports, people, expertise, and that elusive asset called "capacity."

We hear it from almost everyone we talk to who works in K–12 education: public schools have been asked to do more with less for too long. It's more than just an everyday complaint or a cop-out. There's evidence that this continued "making do" is more than just a source of stress for educators. It's also significantly undercutting effectiveness and equity in our schools, complicating each of our efforts to serve students and do the work of our profession (see "Facts About Resources").

Although the pandemic led to additional funds for schools, we all know that in the long term, planning for additional resources is most likely misplaced optimism. That reality leaves leaders with the question of how to do more with existing or even shrinking resources.

Facts About Resources

- Students from low-income families who attend better-funded schools are more likely to finish high school and enroll in postsecondary education and less likely to experience poverty as adults (Jackson et al., 2015). As of this writing, the pandemic has created short-term bursts of extra funding, but paperwork, local offsets, and other factors are constraining use.

- About half of public school buildings are in disrepair (Alexander et al., 2014), and even more lack essential infrastructure. We know of one school that called its new SMARTboards "DumbBoards" because the building couldn't handle the electrical load needed to run them all—and forget about the internet. As the principal said, "Instructional practice is stuck in 1980." And, of course, lack of ventilation and space complicated safe reopenings after the pandemic.

- Teacher and principal shortages are placing more underprepared and uncertified educators in schools, especially in those serving high proportions of students with low family incomes or students of color (Learning Policy Institute, 2018).

- School systems struggle to align professional learning and supports with educator needs that are increasingly complex and diverse. Teachers *and* researchers agree that the best professional learning is personalized, job-embedded, sustained, engaged, and relevant and treats educators as professionals (Bill & Melinda Gates Foundation, 2014; Hill, 2007). Surveys show that fewer than a third of educators favorably rate the professional learning they receive based on those evidence-based criteria (Bill & Melinda Gates Foundation, 2014).

- Fifty-three percent of public school students are of color. Despite evidence that diversifying the teacher workforce leads to better outcomes for those students, the profession has grown *less* diverse since the early 2000s (Goldhaber et al., 2020).

Even so, the United States is investing significant resources in education. How much money does the nation spend each year on public elementary and secondary schools? Don't do an online search to find the answer. Just take a guess and write it down. If you want to know, the answer is at the end of the chapter on page 67. Let's put that number in context. If the amount of money were the entire gross domestic product (GDP) of a country, the amount the United States spends on public preK–12 education alone would be the 20th largest GDP in the world—just ahead of the GDP of Switzerland (World Bank, 2020).

Challenges and Shifts

Even with the significant investment the United States makes in education, resources and related capacity can still seem scarce. However, as shown in Figure 4.1, we can change how we think about resources in at least three ways.

FIGURE 4.1

Leadership Shifts for Resources and Capacity

Moving from . . .	Shifting to . . .
What we have	How we use what we have
Waiting for more	Moving ahead without more
Silver bullets and patches	Game changers

What We Have → How We Use What We Have

The fact is, if we want to get serious about goals for transforming public education—or even just meet our annual improvement targets—we have to make decisions based on what's best for teaching and learning, not on what's already implemented or budgeted. Otherwise, we'll continue directing our available resources to all the wrong places in a futile attempt to reach our goals. To accomplish what we want to achieve, we need to frame resource questions differently.

If you're thinking, *Sure, but we can't just make the budget and staff bigger or the day longer,* you're right. The good news is that it's possible to address our resource and capacity needs more effectively even if we can't add more. (In fact, sometimes "adding more" is exactly the wrong answer—but we'll come back to that later.)

Maybe you know—or you are—one of those principals who is always able to stretch the budget a little further, keeps staff for years, and rarely seems overwhelmed or burnt out by the juggling act of school leadership. Or perhaps you're a teacher leader who manages to mentor colleagues and build great results and relationships for students and is the one who's always got to be in the room or on the Zoom call if the team's going to make a major leap.

These educators aren't magicians. They're masters of reallocation, which has emerged as a key strategy in school improvement (Plecki et al., 2006). And although their work and contexts are always unique, they have a few strategies in common to get past the barriers that resource constraints place on them and their teams.

Waiting for More → Moving Ahead Without More

Again, we acknowledge that school leaders can't control every factor. The size of district budgets, timing of budget cycles, demands of grants or collective bargaining agreements, or staffing allocations are what they are. Effective school leaders have made one critical adaptive shift: understanding that while they may not control everything, that doesn't mean they and their staff and colleagues have no control at all.

School leaders who make this shift begin to see opportunities in schedules and budgets to prioritize what is most important. Schools will never have unlimited resources, so where we allocate our time, money, and facilities indicates where priorities are situated. Later in the chapter we will highlight some of the strategies school leaders who have made this shift are using, but the fundamental issue is to stop waiting for more resources and use the time, talent, and treasure available to us to move forward in ways that prioritize what we value most. Doing so necessarily means that teachers and administrators have to engage with one another to identify what is best for students.

Silver Bullets and Patches → Game Changers

Context always matters when addressing adaptive challenges—challenges that require a change in mindset because the problem and solution are not initially clear (Heifetz, 1994). Mindful use of resources is where theoretical ideas meet the reality of real-world challenges.

As leaders, we can become defensive about why we have not engaged particular adaptive challenges or have not seen the success we desired when we have engaged. When we observe other schools and districts that are making adaptive improvement, we tend to dismiss their success with phrases like "Our district is not big enough to do that," "Our district is too big to do that," or "They don't have students like ours." In many cases, school and district contexts are more alike than we think. For example, students in urban schools might be closer to resources such as museums, cultural events, and other learning opportunities, but if they are not aware of or able to access them, they do not receive any more benefit than students in rural schools who are not near those resources.

Although we agree there are no silver bullets or automatic right answers, we do know that collective leadership gives us game-changing approaches to aligning our school's work with its goals. Collective leadership consists of the collective experiences and expertise of a school team, often further enriched by students, families, and communities that add perspectives, social capital, and solutions. Returning to an example we described in Chapter 1, in one large urban high school in Illinois, a team of teachers, administrators, students, and parents met monthly to improve the school culture through a Positive Behavioral Intervention and Supports (PBIS) program. The principal attended but did not lead the meeting; he was present to offer feedback and determine ways to reallocate resources needed to support their efforts. With no additional resources and over the course of several years, the school significantly reduced office referrals, changed hallway behaviors, almost eliminated school fights, and achieved national PBIS recognition.

Again, this improvement was not contingent on resources beyond three teachers having a common planning period and a principal willing to reallocate some existing resources. It also wasn't dependent on the school's context. As we'll show in our case study of Walker-Gamble Elementary later in this chapter, small, rural, preK–5 schools can apply the same approaches to get results. What matters is using those approaches to apply the collective expertise and wisdom already within schools to create better, more aligned solutions (Eckert, 2018).

Explicating the Challenges and Shifts

Resources matter—and here's the one that matters most. Salaries and benefits account for approximately 70 percent of most school budgets. Therefore, if we are going to use financial resources more effectively, we have to consider how we pay teachers and administrators. In a district, collectively examining what educators' contracts and pay scales incentivize—experience, learning, performance—is a useful exercise. Doing that in isolation or in a top-down manner is unlikely to result in an innovative or useful solution (see "Seven Steps to a Better Contract").

Seven Steps to a Better Contract

The following guidelines (Eckert et al., 2018) were developed with districts that undergo collective bargaining in mind, but they are useful to shape approaches to *any* reevaluation of how a district or school sets up incentives (including compensation) for how educators use their time and expertise. In our work with Mira Education and its partners, we have used these successfully in a range of district contexts and sizes.

Take time to work together. Begin early with a team of administrators and teachers who start the process by identifying what is working in the district that compensation could more effectively support and what could be catalyzed through more strategic compensation. Meeting monthly over the course of 18 to 24 months should provide enough time to develop a strong plan.

Don't bargain—recommend. If the team of administrators is freed from entrenched positions that appear during contract negotiations, then the team can simply make a recommendation that can expedite and improve the contract.

Look internally to identify strengths and face reality. When administrators and teachers have candid conversations about strengths and budget realities, they can identify innovative improvements that break through the walls created by a lack of communication and limited understanding.

Look externally for improvement, not silver-bullet solutions. With more than 98,000 school districts in the United States, there are plenty of opportunities to learn from others about what might be an improved framework. No system or compensation model is a perfect solution; but certainly, others' innovations can provide frameworks for contextualized improvement.

Establish shared values. Working as a district team of teachers and administrators, identifying nonnegotiables and core values is essential to honest dialogue. Celebrating what is shared and identifying where views differ build a foundation from which to construct a better contract.

Communicate with others. A relatively small, representative team creates opportunities for conversations where everyone can effectively contribute to the dialogue. However, this approach requires each member of the team to collect feedback regularly from those they represent.

Trust the process and one another. Vulnerability is necessary to develop trust (Brown, 2018). Trust is an essential element of school improvement (Bryk & Schneider, 2002). Particularly when considering how to use compensation more strategically, trust is essential and must be built over time, with work grounded in the integrity of the team.

Moving beyond salaries and benefits, the ways we use technology, build schedules, use facilities, and direct our energy reflect what we prioritize. We cannot and do not want to say yes to everything. Doing so will typically lead to abandoning the work later because we are overwhelmed or too impatient to realize changes. Deliberately leaving behind ideas that are not core to our mission is such an important practice that it has a name: organized abandonment (Eckert, 2017).

For example, technology is a tool that can be used to enhance the talents of teachers and administrators to better serve student learning. Identifying technology that enhances student engagement, communication, assessment, and feedback can help support the mission of a school. Tools such as Flipgrid, Pear Deck, Gimkit, and Mural and their successors have free versions that can be extremely useful to teachers and students—as long as schools do not adopt too many at once or mandate their use in a top-down manner (Eckert, 2020).

Similarly, the way we design the work of teachers and administrators demonstrates what we prioritize. Does a school value collaboration, collective problem solving, reflection, and improvement? Look at the way it designs work days, weeks, and years for teachers and administrators. Is there time built into teachers' schedules to see one another teach? Are they able to give each other feedback on how to improve? Do administrators and teachers participate together in professional learning? These are all questions that do not necessarily require additional resources; they just require a school to evaluate and then creatively design how it organizes work and time.

The design of learning spaces can also indicate what schools value. At a school just outside of Syracuse, New York, the teachers and administrators got to design a renovated version of an older middle school building. They created pods of classrooms for each grade level of teams that could flexibly connect 24, 48, 72, or 96 students in varying configurations. Small spaces in the hallway allowed students or students and teachers to collaborate. The learning spaces were bright and open (Eckert & Butler, 2021).

The opportunity for teachers and administrators to design a building together is not a luxury that most will have, but there is a lot that they can do with existing spaces. Are there flexible spaces for teachers to meet in smaller groups with students? Are there designated spaces for teachers to meet with other teachers and administrators?

Within the overall context, the most significant resources in any school for improving outcomes for students are the teachers and administrators in that building (Branch et al., 2012; Hanushek & Rivkin, 2012; Kane & Staiger, 2008; Leithwood et al., 2004; Leithwood & Mascall, 2008; Rivkin et al., 2005). How are we developing and supporting their capacity? Are we using their time and expertise well? Walker-Gamble Elementary offers some insights.

Sustainable Schedules and Solutions: Walker-Gamble Elementary

Walker-Gamble Elementary is located in a small rural community in South Carolina along Interstate 95. This area of South Carolina has been dubbed the "Corridor of Shame" due to the underresourcing of the schools (Ferillo, 2005). Yet in 2020, Walker-Gamble received South Carolina's top recognition for schools, the Palmetto's Finest award, and it has made strides in narrowing achievement gaps among its students. How did it do this?

In 2016, first-year principal Allen Kirby, in keeping with three out of four U.S. principals, recognized that the role of the principal was too complex to do alone (MetLife, 2013). He needed the collective strength of the entire staff of 37 educators at Walker-Gamble to improve. At the time, 41 percent of the students met or exceeded state standards in literacy and 52 percent met the standards in math (South Carolina Department of Education, 2016). Although these scores were above the state average, the staff recognized that the students were capable of significant improvement.

Despite a strong culture and social ties in the school, teachers had little opportunity to build professional relationships that allowed them to share a common language around instructional practice, observe one another's teaching, engage in shared learning and improvement efforts, or make sound decisions based on data—all research-based best practices for improving collective efficacy, instructional quality, and student learning.

By 2019, Walker-Gamble's needs, resources, and staff hadn't changed; but how the school used what it had—and the extent to which innovation and best practice were leading to results—had changed markedly. Every student and educator set data-informed personalized learning goals at least quarterly. Three-quarters of the students experienced one-to-one instruction. Grade-level PLCs met weekly to conduct learning walks and assess what works. Every teacher had at least five hours of dedicated professional learning and collaboration time each week. Student grade retentions had decreased, and teachers had reported improvements in collective efficacy, a leading factor in student achievement growth (Donohoo et al., 2018). Walker-Gamble participated in the pilot cohort of the SC Collective Leadership Initiative (see "The SC Collective Leadership Initiative"), which included learning modules that built knowledge of continuous-improvement processes and strategies to reallocate existing resources around specific student needs, opportunities to share promising practices with other schools, and monthly coaching to help the school's leadership team examine and respond to impact data.

The SC Collective Leadership Initiative

The South Carolina Department of Education partnered with Mira Education to develop a statewide Collective Leadership Initiative (CLI), intended to engage teams of leaders within schools to lead changes that help students meet the Profile of the SC Graduate. Twelve schools participated in the pilot during 2017–18, with districtwide expansion in one local education agency (Clarendon District 3, home of Walker-Gamble Elementary) in 2018–19. Between 2019 and 2022, 29 additional schools joined CLI, with school teams identifying a "problem of practice" to address through collective leadership. During the cohort experience, school teams learn from and with one another, analyze efficacy and conditions data, develop action plans, and reflect on the impact of their collective leadership work. The year culminates in a Showcase, where progress and learning are shared with one another and publicly.

Below are a few key findings from a survey on collective teacher efficacy that staff at Walker-Gamble have completed 14 times since 2018. Regardless of the time of year, the results have been remarkably consistent and significantly better than those from other strong schools in their CLI cohort. Of the respondents, 77 percent agree that they are "leaders beyond my classroom." On all 14 survey administrations, the following percentages of educators indicated they agree or strongly agree with the survey item in quotation marks:

- 96 percent are "satisfied with my current job."
- 91 percent report that teachers "value the work" they do at the school or on students' behalf.
- 96 percent report that the principal "values the work" they do at the school or on students' behalf.
- 94 percent report that students "value the work" they do at the school or on students' behalf.
- 98 percent report they are "making a significant educational difference in the lives of the students at my school."
- 96 percent believe that "if I try really hard, I can make progress with even the most unmotivated students."
- 98 percent can "work well with any teacher at this school."

- 94 percent report that "teachers and administrators at this school can solve most any problem, no matter how difficult."

By using resources wisely and building capacity through collective leadership that catalyzes the work of others, Walker-Gamble has built collective efficacy that is sustainable through pandemics, local challenges, and external pressures.

Like many schools, Walker-Gamble was data-rich and information-poor. Although the staff were frustrated with stagnant achievement levels, looking at their data simply increased the pressure; it didn't help them maximize learning time for students and educators within the confines of traditional staffing and scheduling modules. Through the CLI design process, the team learned strategies to identify root causes of challenges showing up in school data and set key improvement goals around which to better use resources. Here are the strategies they adopted.

Prioritizing the amount and quality of instructional time in each day's schedule. Teachers regularly complained about not having uninterrupted time to meet state-mandated Read to Succeed minutes or to complete focused lessons because schedules were driven by "pull-outs and IEP meetings and trying to get everyone through gym and the lunchroom," explained Assistant Principal Nancy Moore. Staff completed microcredentials that helped them assess how they used time. They discovered their master schedule prioritized everything *except* unbroken blocks of time for instruction. In response, a team of teachers and administrators reconfigured schedules around blocks of uninterrupted instructional time each morning and afternoon for every grade level. Related arts periods, recess, lunch, and supplemental instruction were placed back-to-back rather than scattered through the day. The new plan resulted in reaching or exceeding targets for Read to Succeed, and it provided time for follow-through on differentiated instruction.

Driving literacy growth for every student by offering targeted, differentiated instruction for key subgroups. Facilitated PLC coaching cycles and meetings emphasize individual goal setting, guiding teachers through processes for their own professional growth that are adapted for use with students (especially English learners, gifted and talented students, and students "approaching" standards). Weekly one-hour sessions in a Personalized Learning Lab give students time for targeted follow-up through gamified and hands-on learning experiences; online assessment offers real-time data on progress to guide the next day's work. With more predictable instructional time available, teachers were in a better position to plan and execute differentiated strategies for subgroups that were key to equity and improvement goals.

Encouraging collaborative learning practices among teachers. Walker-Gamble always enjoyed a warm and supportive culture. Attention is now given to structuring the professional side of those relationships to grow practice and student learning. Professional learning communities engage in learning walks, allowing teachers to take part in reciprocal observations with colleagues several times each nine weeks. Common planning periods for each grade level guarantee that colleagues can work together daily. Twenty-two teachers and administrators completed microcredentials that built their competencies for better use of instructional time and resources. Superintendent Connie Dennis joined one team in completing micro-credentials, extending shared learning and practice to the district office.

Engaging teachers as coleaders of change and professional learning in the building. Repurposing title funding and existing personnel allocations allowed Walker-Gamble to create two "hybrid" teacher-leader roles, which combine direct instruction in classrooms and a STEAM lab with time to serve on the instructional leadership team and support colleagues. The media specialist role has expanded to support gifted and talented students. In addition, the school has eliminated typical fully released coach and specialist positions, consolidating traditional standalone positions to make space for flexible full-time-equivalent (FTE) positions that wrap around school and student needs.

Walker-Gamble educators are quick to underscore that collective leadership "isn't something extra that we 'do.'" Teacher leader Amanda Williamson says, "It's just become the way we do our work now." Maintaining this mindset—and ensuring that the design of collectively led efforts integrates and amplifies what already works well—avoids overloading already busy educators.

Strategies to Support the Shifts

Improvement requires the collective expertise of a team of school leaders who understand but are not constrained by existing resources and capacity. In the next sections, you will find strategies and related tools that will help your team consider better use of resources and existing capacity.

Strategy 1: Reimagine Your Resources

As we mentioned earlier, collective leadership is more about embracing a process than implementing a program. Various tools have proven to be successful in providing context-specific data for educators to analyze and then act upon. For example, making mindful use of an existing resource starts with understanding your priorities, then examining how that resource is being used and to what degree it is aligned to your priorities. Gaps or misalignment suggest places to reexamine use of resources.

Schools' ability to shift spending can vary widely, but *every* school sets schedules, arranges assigned staff, and makes other decisions about how time is spent in meetings, professional learning, and similar activities. These elements add up to the single biggest budget line for schools whether you see them in your budget software or not. We focus here on how to spend time in ways that align your school's capacity with its goals. Using the tools we provide, you can rethink how you are using time in your school and how you might adjust your in-class time and the master schedule to better meet the needs of your students.

Begin by determining where you are currently allocating resources. We noted at the start of the book that collective leadership is intended not to be a program but to help you and your team make strategic sense of programs and possibly even to eliminate those that no longer align with your goals for yourselves and your students. The following activity protocol can help you take on that task. You and your team will need up to 90 minutes for this work. Here are the steps to follow:

1. **Recall the vision** (5 minutes). To begin, remind everyone of the vision and strategy: What are the big goals or aims that guide everything your team will do? (If this is not clear, visit Chapter 2 for framing and suggestions to develop this before you move ahead.)

2. **Set the stage** (5 minutes). Explain the steps you're about to take as a team to clarify what you will start, continue, and stop doing.

3. **List your programs** (15 minutes). As a team, create a list of all the programs or other initiatives you are currently implementing. Consider curriculum, professional learning, and other efforts. The list-making process should create a visible artifact for the team, so for in-person meetings, consider having everyone post ideas on a whiteboard or chart paper. For virtual meetings, you can use a Google Doc, Padlet, or other collaborative software. If time is tight, you can set up the activity in one meeting and then do it asynchronously in advance of the next meeting.

4. **Sort your list** (20 minutes). Once your list is compiled, sort each program you listed by the goal(s) or element(s) of your vision it satisfies. Ideally, you can manipulate your list to move aligned items together. Which might not satisfy *any* goals? Which satisfy *multiple* goals? Flag each visually.

5. **Assess the impact** (20 minutes). Now review each of the "bucketed" lists. Which of the programs for each goal or focus area is giving you the greatest return on your effort? If the list is short and your team is small, you may be able to hold a simple facilitated conversation. For larger groups, consider using a two-stage dot-down process. Each person gets a certain number of dots to rate which programs yield the greatest impact on goals (red), require the least complexity or effort for your team (green), and maximize other resources (blue). This process will give you a relatively quick visual for the return on investment for each item.

6. **Make decisions** (25 minutes). Based on the data you now have, which programs make sense to continue? To double down on? Which might be out of alignment with your goals or require too much energy for the return they bring your staff and students?

Strategy 2: Encourage Collaborative Learning Practices Among Teachers

Consider how the schedule and use of personnel can support efforts to address your priority area(s). We know that when teachers collaborate, students benefit (Jackson & Bruegmann, 2009; Kraft & Papay, 2016; Ronfeldt et al., 2015; Rosenholtz, 1989), so designing the schedule so that teachers have time to work with one another on articulated priorities is likely to drive the improvements school teams intend.

At Walker-Gamble, educators decided that creating a schedule that allowed for uninterrupted instructional time was a priority. As a result, they scheduled that uninterrupted time, then added in the other things that needed to be part of the schedule, such as related arts and lunch.

As you consider your team's priorities, use a format like the one in Figure 4.2 to begin building a schedule that aligns and allows time for educators to collaborate. Start by adding your team's highest-priority items to the schedule. Then build the rest of the schedule around those priorities.

Creating time in the regular school day for educators to collaborate is a first step toward encouraging collaborative learning practices. Once educators have the time to collaborate, they are likely also to need supports and

FIGURE 4.2
A Reimagined School Schedule

Schedule for AY:	Priorities:		
Grade Level	**Start Time**	**Lunch**	**End Time**

structures to build their *capacity* for collaboration. For tools related to building capacity for collaboration, visit the Mira Education website to access additional resources.

Strategy 3: Engage Teachers as Coleaders of Change and Professional Learning

Reallocating resources so that teachers can colead improvement efforts is likely to increase ownership of those efforts and eliminate the need for buy-in. People will own what they help to create.

One way to create time for teachers to lead without leaving their classrooms is to create hybrid positions as Walker-Gamble did. A zero-cost way to do this is to rethink 1.0 FTEs as two 0.5 FTEs. For instance, if an educator in a full-time position does *not* have classroom responsibilities (e.g., a coach or a facilitator), that position can be broken into two 0.5 positions. If you do the same for a full-time classroom position, you could create two hybrid positions, with an educator spending half the time teaching and half leading.

Here are some questions to consider as you think about engaging teachers as coleaders of improvement:

- What opportunities and flexibilities exist for your team to reallocate resources and create opportunities for teachers to have the time and space to colead improvement efforts?
- Are you able to reallocate financial resources to create more hybrid positions?
- Are you able to adjust job descriptions to allow for individuals to combine two 0.5 positions into a 1.0 position?
- Are there other ways beyond the creation of hybrid roles to create time for teachers to colead improvement efforts?

Although the ability of schools to rethink the use of resources varies by state and district, nearly all have at least some flexibility. Find out what those flexibilities are, and then find colleagues who are using resources creatively and discuss their processes. And don't assume that just because "that's the way we've always done it" there are policies that *require* you to follow precedent. Although additional resources can be helpful, more mindful use of the resources you already have at your disposal can also have a powerful impact on improvement efforts.

Wayfinding Summary

Resources and capacity are stretched thin in public schools. To improve, teachers and administrators need to consider how to use what is available, recognize that they will likely move ahead without more, and identify game changers that prioritize instructional time. The following essential ideas from this chapter connect with related strategies and shifts described elsewhere in the book:

- Developing a shared vision and strategy (Chapter 2) ensures that limited time, expertise, and funds can rightly focus on the most important elements of your improvement and innovation work.
- The biggest resource any school, district, or other team has is the time and expertise of its staff. Maximizing the work designs (Chapter 8) that provide optimal opportunities for administrators and teachers to grow is an essential part of using resources well.
- Traditionally, resource decisions are often made exclusively by administrators. However, sharing influence (Chapter 6) on these decisions between teachers and administrators can result in transparency that leads to more effective decisions, greater understanding about "tough calls," and improved relationships among the staff.

Answer to the question on page 52: As of the time of publication, the most recent federal estimates show the United States spends $738.5 billion on public elementary and secondary schools (National Center for Education Statistics, 2020).

5

Strategies, Not Sentiments: Developing Supportive Social Norms and Working Relationships to Build Culture and Continuity

Have you ever been in a meeting that includes a "parking lot activity"? The parking lot provides space to chart thoughts that aren't on the agenda. The intention is to honor ideas, questions, and concerns by setting them aside for another time while not straying from the meeting's focus.

Although it is not certain how this activity originated, chances are it grew out of what we have come to understand about "parking lot meetings"—you know, the meeting after the meeting. The one where ideas, questions, and concerns often get aired with a colleague (or a few) in a different space. The one that happens because there may not be clear expectations around communication norms or perhaps the relationships among the participants are not aligned in a way that allows them to follow those clearly defined norms. Parking lot conversations can operate at extremes in terms of their effects: airing of grievances or playing with new ideas. One is actively destructive to culture, and the other promotes a sense of belonging, innovative space, shared leadership, and possibility. The question is, how do we encourage candor and bring the parking lot into our meeting space? We know clarity of communication and purpose is essential in all sectors, including education (Baldoni, 2009; Duarte, 2020).

A few years ago, Mira Education was working with a district team made up of representative roles: school board and community members, the superintendent, central office leaders, union leaders, building-level administrators, and teachers. The team members brought with them to the meeting rooms an array of interests, filters, concerns, needs, and wants. What made them unique compared with other such teams who encompass a similar range of responsibilities and roles? Not much. The dynamics of communication loops or funnels or tunnels are complicated, particularly in a system that is working to redesign or redefine its hierarchy in some way. Even with the clearest of visions and strategies and the most supportive administrators at all levels, communication can be (and often is) challenging.

Even if the vision and strategy have been clearly set, the administration is intent on being supportive, and adequate resources are in place (as addressed in the previous three chapters), creating a safe, sustainable space, because candidly "clear is kind" communication does not just happen on its own. None of these conditions will accomplish the intended impact without productive relationships built on trust (Bryk & Schneider, 2002; Hargreaves & O'Connor, 2018; Van Velsor & McCauley, 2004). Leadership (shared or not) cannot be effective if there is no followership, no one who aspires to contribute. Although we most often allocate attention to the role of the "leaders" among an assembly of teams such as the one described earlier, the collective contributions of *all* team members demand no less attention if the desired outcome is indeed to draw upon the individual assets each person brings to the table. The balance of "deciding and doing" should flex to the roles and skills represented in the team's collective expertise.

As a result, leaders who engage directly with classroom practitioners around an innovative design project or to tackle a problem of practice at the systems level should consider this different context and the demands it may require for a different approach to "being in the room" or "on the team." Part of this approach might include more intently focusing on those who have informal leadership roles or perhaps do not view themselves as leaders at all (Smylie & Denny, 1990). The dynamics of being side-by-side with formal leaders—perhaps for the first time or only on rare occasions—also require getting acclimated to this shift in leadership practice. A team approach of this nature allows for a different pathway of relationships and decisional structures. This "new way" need not be at the expense of existing connections; ideally, it adds value and depth to those connections toward shared goals. (See Chapter 8 for more about work design.)

We know that effective communications directly connect to and influence relationships and performance, and calibration of how well and how consistently team members communicate is increasingly finding its way into research on high-performing teams (Hong Bui et al., 2019). In team dynamics, identifying challenges and directly addressing them prove to be effective toward advancing the work—and not taking the work to the parking lot. (Read more about this orientation toward improvement in Chapter 7.) This desire and action to get better does not happen in a vacuum; it requires an affective component to be candid and compassionate.

Challenges and Shifts

Although a focus on the work as the priority sounds like a logical approach, we do not have the luxury of isolating an innovative or transformational change to content only. A thriving community of practice involves taking risks and learning alongside one another. And this is made possible with strong working relationships that are multifaceted: one to one, team to team, roles alike, common interests. These webs of communication drive decisions and design cocreated by people who need to deliberate and discern what's best to try first (or not at all); so understanding what team members who bring diverse experiences to the table are thinking (and why) is critical to the success of the work and its odds for sustainability.

Our experiences have led us to suggest at least three necessary shifts for team members charged with navigating complex design and implementation work as part of a collective approach (see Figure 5.1).

Although this short list is not all-inclusive when it comes to the dynamics of establishing and maintaining productive norms and relationships for teams, successfully implementing these three shifts will contribute to a stronger culture for working alongside colleagues. None of these challenges require us to abandon our professional identities, including identities or

FIGURE 5.1

**Leadership Shifts for Supportive Social Norms
and Working Relationships**

Moving from . . .	Shifting to . . .
Unclear, unspoken, or one-way communications that stall a culture of learning and leadership	Agreed-upon norms that engender trusting relationships
Positions and titles that splinter a sense of responsibility for outcomes	Team identity coalesced around a shared purpose
Primary/individual role behavior	Team-member persona

roles we hold as formal leaders or managers within our schools or teams.
Rather, they are about shifting *how we show up* as leaders so we can continue
to invite others into leadership work with us. These shifts that leadership
team members (may need to) develop or more strongly lean into can cultivate even stronger relationships and deeper impact on the work.

Unclear, Unspoken, or One-Way Communications That Stall a Culture of Learning and Leadership → Agreed-Upon Norms That Engender Trusting Relationships

As your team identity is formed, how will your communication and relationships advance and sustain the work of the team? No two teams are the
same, and the unique dynamics of each one require constant attention to
norming and revisiting communications, which form the foundation of the
relationships among members. Whereas innovative work is often complex,
the relationships of those owning the work can also often be complicated—
particularly without due attention to *how* the work is communicated. Every
organization has a communication culture, whether it has been deliberately developed, benignly ignored, or constantly calibrated. Here are three
extremely important watch-fors as teams invest time in focusing on communication norms—an investment well worth making:

Are you being unclear? As Brené Brown (2018) shared in *Dare to Lead*,
"Clear is kind. Unclear is unkind" (p. 48). Often our attempts to spare
unpleasant feelings or responses from team members can backfire. Tiptoeing
around an issue with vaguely subtle messaging may lead not only to not

resolving the issues at hand but perhaps making them even worse. Rarely do problems just "solve themselves," even if they have been acknowledged. And some team members are more astute at subtlety than others. Being clear gives everyone an opportunity to come to agreement on expectations, with less room for confusion or splintering visions or strategies. So, be kind by being clear.

Are you relying on the unspoken? Perhaps even more challenging than being unclear is relying on the unspoken. If phrases like "Well, you all know what I mean" are being shared, chances are there are a number of people in the room who just aren't going to speak up with "Well, no, I don't." And chances are there are multiple people in the room thinking, "Well, I think I know" or "I thought I did, but now I'm not sure." Instead of leaving thoughts to individuals, just say what you mean. And then check for understanding or improving the idea.

Is the "talking part" of communication heavily one-way? As Lyndon B. Johnson once said, "You aren't learning anything when you're talking." Team conversations that norm toward many voices in the room contributing to the analysis and strategies of the work represent collective leadership at its best. A diversity of perspectives, contributions, and ownership is more likely to inform innovation and breakthrough thinking to advance the team's learning and success. Those many voices need a balance of airtime for team discussions to authentically represent the actual team and not just a few voices. Practice a healthy proportion of active listening alongside adding to the discussion, and draw in the voices of less comfortable colleagues who may be hesitant to speak up without encouragement.

Positions and Titles That Splinter a Sense of Responsibility for Outcomes → Team Identity Coalesced Around a Shared Purpose

Positions and titles are important. They bring a sense of order to a system. And no organization is truly "flat"; otherwise, what's there to organize? Being connected and comfortable with the identity of one's position or title is a necessity. This comfort can become a liability, however, when someone is asked to play the role of team member. Yet it can also be a strength. Recognizing not only what you are bringing to the team's table but also what you are *not* bringing is important. Just as critical is understanding what and how others on the team have seen you operate in the past. What role are you known for playing? What work are you noted for doing or having done? Is your identity "in a box" that will need to be redefined? Although you do not need to know answers to all these questions coming into teamwork, you will need to factor these questions of perception into your thinking and behaviors as a team member. And what will ultimately best serve your team will be to focus more on what you contribute to your team's identity, depending on what's needed in a given context, rather than predictably carrying your title or position into every team setting, regardless of the context. Let's look at how assuming a particular persona can best serve the work.

Primary/Individual Role Behavior → Team-Member Persona

As you reflect on your individual identity, you're one step closer to recognizing how you might best shift or lean into both recognized and unknown skills and expertise to best serve the work. Although you may have been brought into a team because of some specific content knowledge you possess or your responsibilities in the organization, it will be important not to be limited by that identity. How might you grow beyond the expected contributions? What expertise or experience can you contribute that has yet to be tapped or recognized by your colleagues? In what ways might you push beyond your own comfort zone to grow and learn alongside your colleagues?

Experimenting with "role switching" within team settings and encouraging others to do so may allow your team to land on new and innovative approaches to old and distracting issues. Positioning your role in a different team space could be the impetus for new team thinking. In short, one norm worth embracing is to be open to shifting the normal. (Doing this will require not only building up your personal capacity for this flexibility—the focus of this chapter—but also may require you to think differently about how work is structured for you and your team so that you can more readily share the work of leadership. See Chapter 8 for more on that complementary approach.)

Let's take a look at one school that prioritized creating a healthy culture focused on establishing social norms and trusting relationships.

Creating Learners and Leaders Among All: Midland Valley Preparatory School

Founded in 2002 in Graniteville, South Carolina, as Midland Valley Preparatory School, with a small student population ranging from preK through 6th grade, the growing public charter school is now called Horse Creek Academy (HCA). Its 120 staff members serve approximately 1,250 students, preK through 11th grade. Ann Marie Taylor has positioned her role as "HCA Lead Learner"—otherwise called the principal in most schools. Created to provide parents and students with "a worthy choice in free public education," HCA is a highly sought-after choice for educators (with 100 applicants for 10 positions in fall 2022) and students (with almost 900 applicants for 70 slots). Based on the reputation of the school, teachers are seeking a culture that honors their expertise in the classroom and their voices outside the classroom—as contributors who influence the culture and customs that bring the school to life.

This appeal has not always been the case. When Taylor became Lead Learner in the summer of 2019 (shedding the title of principal), she inherited challenges. Recurring leadership changes had contributed to inconsistent direction for the school's vision and future; uneven responsibilities among staff created a fragmented sense of ownership regarding the school's success; and isolated practice affected communications as well as relationships among staff. The "traditional leadership" approach was not working, so she set out to create a culture built upon relationships characterized by high trust and transparency.

How did this happen? In searching for support to address its needs, HCA applied for and became a participating school in the Collective Leadership Initiative (CLI), a project administered by the South Carolina Department of Education in partnership with Mira Education. "We wanted to honor and elevate the idea that teachers were fully capable of making hard decisions and taking on leadership roles schoolwide. We wanted to highlight that administrators were willing to do everything teachers were doing," Taylor said, citing her top reason for joining CLI.

To create such a shift in the leadership structure of the school, early conversations among staff primarily focused on establishing shared norms and expectations. Soon those conversations moved from HCA staff to also include parents, students, and community members. These discussions led to another shift in HCA culture: positions and titles that separated leaders and teachers became purposely blurred, and a redefined organizational chart illustrated collective leadership, anchored by a leadership team of 12 teacher leaders. All regularly practice as classroom teachers, including Taylor, who teaches one class each semester to high school students (her two classes in the 2022–23 school year were Criminology and the Psychology of Happiness).

Next in HCA's shift toward collective leadership was realizing the shared vision and shared decision-making norms, developed by staff and stakeholders. "Buy-in comes with builders," Taylor said. Recognizing inclusion in building the process meant shared ownership from inception, resulting in solutions that were co-owned as well. Taylor worked with her team to create a norm-setting protocol for communications to address expectations for all involved in the livelihood of HCA: staff, students, parents, board members, and other community stakeholders. Inclusion in the process also engendered transparency, trust, and rapport, as communications expectations were established. Commitment to the norms became a nonnegotiable responsibility that included specific actions for recommitment as anticipated lapses would occur (and they do). The process also built in frequent opportunities to revisit the norms for a check-in to see if the process was meeting the implementation test for being both pragmatic and consistent. "When we are off the norms, it shows. We must be brave enough to discuss when we are; we have to hold each other accountable at all levels," Taylor said.

As HCA's student population and staff continue to expand, well-grounded communication protocols will help counter some of the growing pains that may come with such growth. A high rate of teacher retention is attributed to this strong culture, which also features an expanding menu of leadership opportunities for teachers to lead and teach. Taylor understands that authentic collective leadership serves to buffer each shift and in many cases creates opportunity for growth with each one.

As the leadership team has worked together for the past couple of years, the vision is becoming more focused, even as it expands. What began as "forced coverage" of "areas other than my own" (brought on by pandemic-related demands and interruptions in staff availability) has become support for the full range of student grades and staff assignments, tapping into the potential power of relationships. From the front office staff to those who oversee the canteen, from every classroom to all parents, "crossing over" to space other than "my norm" is being encouraged and held up as the next space to deepen the commitment to the relational culture of HCA.

Learning to take on multiple identities as an individual and team member has contributed to the successful culture of HCA that is attracting so many educators and students. And the team is continuing to grow in its reach and impact. The next growth and "identity expansion" includes "new learning for all adults to engage across all grade levels." The rationale for doing so is that getting "out of their boxes" and into new spaces will deepen school-wide commitment among all staff. "You can't have an all-in mentality if you engage in just one thing," Taylor said.

Strategies to Support the Shifts

In Mira Education engagements around system redesign, we stipulate that team members who will be planning, analyzing, leading, and implementing the work should represent a cross-section of roles within the system. Most often this includes teachers in all types of roles and contexts, as well as administrators and other personnel in leadership or policymaking roles—all wearing the same hat of a "team member." Initially, some of those hats fit more comfortably than others. For formal leaders, recognizing that their titles may loom larger than they realize can be an important filter to bring to a team culture. Although each person has one seat at the table, formal leaders may just be taking up more space than others. And those not serving in formal leadership capacities can sense that space, even if it is not intentionally brought to the table (and it is almost impossible not to bring it).

Given what we know about the influence communications has on the work itself, how do we each bring unique communication styles into a room and become productive members of a team? One way is to begin the work of the team by discussing how the team should and will communicate rather than talking about the work itself. If this happens at all, it is often *only* at the launch of a project, or just with new team members, or when a misunderstanding arises, or work gets off track, or confusion becomes evident. Productive communications, just like healthy relationships, require constant attention.

Strategy 1: Establish and Maintain Equitable and Inclusive Norms and Protocols for Communications

How do teams go about establishing and maintaining communications protocols and norms that ensure the work of the team is equitable and inclusive? The tool in Figure 5.2 offers a starting point.

Needing to react and rebuild clear communications can be much more difficult than establishing clear protocols at the onset to keep communications under control. Keeping communications under control means staying keenly aware of what is happening (or not) in the room. Is there clear evidence of agency, equity of voice, stepping up and stepping back, adhering to the group's agreed-upon norms? Tuning in to both verbal and nonverbal elements in team communications can often help teams avoid straying too far from unproductive communications, as can having a planned protocol in place if and when an issue or breakdown in team dynamics needs to be addressed.

FIGURE 5.2

A Tool for Establishing Norms and Protocols for Equitable and Inclusive Communication

Directions: As you and your colleagues convene for a first team meeting, consider how to establish norms and protocols for communicating and then proceed to establish them. Use this tool to guide your thinking. You may choose to have non-role-alike members in small groups generating responses to the questions below. Once discussion is complete (about 10 minutes), ask each group to share their ideas about the how. Post up the ideas, including duplicates, so that the whole group can review and revise. Come to consensus on what "makes the list"—the how.

Grounding principles: How will we work together to craft our norms for this team's work? How will we ensure that we are being clear, saying what we mean, and engaging in multidirectional communication?

Execution: Next, move to the what. Execute the agreed-upon strategy.

Norms: What norms will we use to inform and guide our work, both during and between meetings?

Post, publish, and revisit the norms at the beginning of each meeting.

Strategy 2: Revisit Team Norms

What is the proactive plan for when (not if) some aspect of team dynamics becomes unbalanced, sluggish, uninspired? The tool in Figure 5.3 allows team members to examine their individual team personas, contributions to the work, adherence to the norms, and commitments for recalibration of the team's collective responsibilities. Use it to check on and recalibrate norms. A bimonthly review is recommended. This tool addresses to what extent

FIGURE 5.3

A Tool for Revisiting Norms

Directions: Use this reflection tool to check in on your norms and to what extent they are working for you and your colleagues. Respond to the following questions individually, and then share your responses with your team. Be sure to adjust and adapt your work as needed.

To what extent do you agree or disagree with the following statements?	Strongly Disagree	Disagree	Agree	Strongly Agree	Share insights about your responses.
Our norms are evident in our practices.					
Our norms work well for our team.					
Our norms are focused yet flexible enough to meet the needs of different situations.					

Which norms are working best for you? Provide context for the norm(s) you selected.	Which norms do you wish to revisit because they don't seem to be relevant or working well? Provide context for the norm(s) you selected.

norms are working for your team. Respond to the questions individually and then share whole-group data for discussion and team action regarding the team norms. Reminder: Stay tuned in to the filter of your team persona as you respond to these questions.

Wayfinding Summary

No matter what the context and content of the work are, the relationships among the team members and the culture that thrives (or does not) through those relationships play a decisive role in the success of the team. Clear and predictable modes of communication are at least half the battle of accomplishing the work. Of course, relationships never exist in a vacuum. The chapters specified in the following list explore connections with other collective leadership conditions and strategies:

- Formal titles and positions matter and cannot always be checked at the door of a meeting room. However, practicing supportive administration (Chapter 3) helps suspend the hierarchy to a degree that allows for open, candid, and problem-solving conversations.
- Although the persona of the team matters, so does a deep understanding of each individual and the persona that individual brings to that team's identity. Building shared influence (Chapter 6) helps teams know when and how to leverage individuals' strengths and when to call on shared thinking and expertise.
- Even the best of norms needs to be revisited from time to time (we recommend at least once or twice a year). Doing so supports continuous improvement (Chapter 7), sharpens understanding of the norms, and allows inclusion of new voices that have joined the team.

6

Responsibility, Not Roles: Nurturing Shared Influence Authentically and Organically

A principal with whom we have worked said, "I could tell the teachers what to do and they would do it because they are polite and they respect authority. But that is not collective leadership." This principal also actively dispels myths that teachers and administrators are at odds with one another. She is quite clear that "we are on the same team. When we drop into a learning team meeting, it is not for judgment; it is so that we can work together." In this way, she is taking the next step beyond supportive, catalytic administration (described in Chapter 3): creating a sense of shared influence across every member of the staff, regardless of role.

Emphasizing shared influence and responsibility rather than role means that everyone—teachers and administrators alike—participates to some degree in doing and deciding about work (see Figure 6.1). That does not mean everyone is involved in *every* action or decision. Nor does it mean that teachers are delivering something (e.g., professional development, directives, or mandates) on behalf of someone else in the system. It also does not mean that teachers have influence only on the programmatic and classroom-focused decisions (e.g., deciding how a designated amount of money is to be spent or designing school activities), leaving the management and operational decisions

FIGURE 6.1
Balancing Doing and Deciding

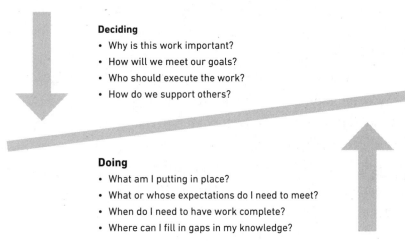

Deciding
- Why is this work important?
- How will we meet our goals?
- Who should execute the work?
- How do we support others?

Doing
- What am I putting in place?
- What or whose expectations do I need to meet?
- When do I need to have work complete?
- Where can I fill in gaps in my knowledge?

and tasks (e.g., budget cuts and instructional issues) to administrators. What it does mean is a balanced way of thinking about how we engage professionals in other roles to make our collective practice stronger. For instance, teachers may be able to offer input into budget decisions by thinking through a classroom-based lens about instructional needs; district administrators will be able to help school-based staff think about the policy and public relations ramifications of how they engage with families and caregivers.

Sharing influence includes taking responsibility for challenges as well as successes, which requires shifts in how teachers and administrators interact with one another and in how they perceive their roles and responsibilities (Day et al. 2004; Lai & Cheung, 2015; Muijs & Harris, 2007). In other words, shared influence is *the condition that arises when teachers and administrators share both work and responsibility for problem solving and leadership across positions and organizational charts.*

This condition is visible in whole new ways as a result of the pandemic experience. With many staffing shortages and quarantines during the pandemic, fully trusting other professionals to share responsibility for outcomes became an everyday occurrence. In addition, education professionals leaned into the trust that was extended to share influence and responsibility.

Education service providers and resource teachers stepped in as long-term subs, and "management by walking around" became impossible due to virtual instruction. As a result of these experiences, we now all have had greater opportunity to understand how critical it is to have leadership within every single classroom.

Extending supportive administration into strategic shared influence happens at the intersection of resources and capacity (Chapter 4), social norms and working relationships (Chapter 5), and work design (Chapter 8). When educators have the skills and resources they need, strong professional relationships with one another, and the structures to be able to do good work together, then the conditions exist for them to learn with and from one another and lead together.

It is important to keep in mind that simply applying technical solutions by buying the books about the latest leadership strategy (resources), developing communication norms (relationships and social norms), and getting educators in a room together (work design) are not likely to yield the shared influence we are talking about. The necessary adaptive shift includes supporting educators to shift their *practices* so that they take action as leaders and deciders who have the ability and opportunity to affect the broader school community and, thereby, student outcomes. The adaptive shift also includes educators shifting their mindset and behaving in ways that are indicative of their leadership ability and decision-making authority.

Although these shifts can be challenging, teachers and administrators working alongside one another will pay dividends that will ultimately benefit students. The shifts described in this chapter provide opportunities for educators to model the behaviors and skills they intend to instill in students. Among those are learning together and from one another, creating a sense of collective ownership, and cultivating a culture of inclusive leadership.

Challenges and Shifts

Educators influence one another in a number of ways in every school, but questions emerge: Is that influence strategic and focused on improvement? Do those who influence others do so in a way that benefits students and the school community, or does that influence erode culture and run counter to improvement? In our work, we have observed that when educators make three shifts and use the strategies we describe in the following text, their influence on one another is focused on improvement (see Figure 6.2).

Isolating Work According to Role → Influencing One Another Across Roles Through Observation

The typical school in the United States consists of a number of classrooms separated from one another by solid walls. Each classroom has a teacher who works with a group of students (typically 25 to 30) on a specific content area for a set period of time. At predictable intervals, either the content changes (usually in elementary schools) or the students move to a different room for different content (typically in middle and high schools).

This egg-crate structure of schools (Wise, 2012) offers few opportunities for educators to learn from and with one another, yet few will dispute the necessity for educators to do so. Even where those opportunities do exist, they often occur *in spite* of the structure of the system, not *because* of it. If we truly value the skills of cooperation and collaboration and the practice of de-siloed work, we must create *systems* that enable that work to occur. The work cannot take place around the edges or be another thing added to educators' already too full plates.

In most cases, the structure and processes within schools are managed by administrators who have very different roles and responsibilities than teachers. The siloing described above replicates itself in the work of teachers

FIGURE 6.2
Leadership Shifts for Shared Influence

Moving from . . .	Shifting to . . .
Isolating work according to role	Influencing one another across roles through observation
Maintaining rigid and discrete spheres of influence that may elicit "pockets of shifts"	Creating dynamic spheres of influence that drive whole-school success
Excluding members of the school community from leadership	Including people with diverse experiences and perspectives in leadership

and administrators. Structures embedded in human resource systems isolate teachers and administrators from one another, despite many administrators having been teachers at some point in their career and wanting to keep themselves grounded in teaching and learning. Because the system is structured to differentiate between the role of teacher and the role of administrator, the conflation of leadership work with the role of administrator has ended up deeply ingrained in the system (as is evident in job descriptions, pay scales, and reporting structures). Those who intend to share influence usually do so in spite of the system, not because of it, as this siloed model has existed across most schools since public schooling in the United States moved beyond the one-room schoolhouse.

Few educators in the United States have the opportunity to watch their colleagues teach or lead (Johnston & Tsai, 2018). Whether we are talking about a teacher watching another teacher, an administrator observing an administrator colleague, or a teacher shadowing an administrator, these opportunities are rare. Even when educators want these types of interactions to occur, they require significant effort and energy to get scheduled and completed because the system is not set up to accommodate this request. Yet this is one of the most powerful ways that educators learn with and from one another. The experience of educators observing one another is also frequently an entry point into teachers seeing themselves as and ultimately taking on the identity of a leader. In fact, many of the CLI schools with which we work started their collective leadership journey by de-siloing the work of teachers, which quickly resulted in more teachers viewing themselves as leaders. In general, 51 percent of teachers nationwide have leadership roles in their schools (MetLife, 2013); but in a 2022 SC Department of Education survey of collective teacher efficacy, more than 71 percent of teachers in CLI schools indicated that they consider themselves leaders.

When educators open their practice to peers, they begin to influence and learn from one another. Peer assistance and review supports improvement in teaching that results in improved student outcomes (Johnson et al., 2010; Papay & Johnson, 2012). Conversing about what they saw and experienced as a result of observing or shadowing is a way that educators influence one another. As this practice is strengthened, it is not at all unusual for the work to organically deepen in the areas that best support students.

Maintaining Rigid and Discrete Spheres of Influence That May Elicit "Pockets of Shifts" → Creating Dynamic Spheres of Influence That Drive Whole-School Success

Margaret Wheatley (2006) has said, "People support what they create. . . . It doesn't matter how brilliant or correct the plan is—it simply doesn't work to ask people to sign on when they haven't been involved in the planning process" (p. 68). Creating structures and processes for teams of educators to broaden and leverage their spheres of influence, make strategic decisions, and design plans for improvement results in a culture where shared influence can thrive.

You wouldn't be reading this if you weren't already interested in and committed to sharing influence and creating a sense of collective responsibility for outcomes. Whether you are working to initiate or to strengthen structures for shared influence, we have learned from educators who have engaged in this work that sharing influence and responsibility for doing and deciding can be challenging, but it pays dividends as schools drive toward their improvement goals. By making this shift, we create an opportunity to cultivate collective ownership for whole-school success.

Let's start with what is likely to be the elephant in the room: When push comes to shove, administrators and those in other formal leadership roles hold positional authority so that even when the intent is to create a collectively led or co-owned climate, words and actions can be perceived as directives. In fact, it is not at all unusual for that to happen. In the strategies section later in this chapter, we identify some specific and explicit actions that formal leaders can take to neutralize power dynamics and support the creation of a climate of shared influence for whole-school success.

Let's not assume that the onus for creating shared influence lies only with administrators. Other staff members also have a responsibility for stepping into the leadership space created for them. Not only do administrators have to be willing to set the stage for shared influence and collective leadership, but teachers must be willing to broaden and leverage their spheres of influence *and* to engage in management activities related to their work and their teams' work. Generally speaking, teachers are accustomed to their primary sphere of influence being within their classroom and perhaps within their grade level or department. Administrators are accustomed to having a much broader sphere of influence that includes the entire school and overlaps with (and in some cases overrides) teachers' classrooms. For collective leadership to take hold, however, those limited and discrete spheres need to be able to shift and be more dynamic based on the current context and needs being addressed. As teachers assume responsibilities for deciding and doing, their sphere of influence will need to grow. And administrators who make space for others to lead may need to use their sphere of influence in different ways. Here are some examples:

- In this chapter's opening story, the principal intentionally and strategically shifted her sphere of influence to allow the growth of the teachers for whom she had set the stage for leadership. She is quick to acknowledge that she *could* tell teachers what to do, but she doesn't so that they can grow their own leadership and sphere of influence.

- A number of schools with which we work have teachers who have expanded their spheres of influence in ways that have resulted in changes to the school schedule, shifts in professional learning, and adjustments to grade-level meetings. These teachers are now influencing not only their classrooms, but also their colleagues and administrators.

Excluding Members of the School Community from Leadership → Including People with Diverse Experiences and Perspectives in Leadership

Addressing inequities that are built into the U.S. education system will require leveraging the talent of all education stakeholders working together, regardless of role. Effective shared influence requires the intentional and strategic inclusion of diverse perspectives and experiences, as well as a nonnegotiable focus on equity. Although having one person be responsible for decision making and holding individuals accountable for outcomes is clear, simple, and efficient, approaching school and district work in this way has not resulted in a more inclusive and equitable system. Instead, it is a classic example of a quote frequently attributed to H. L. Mencken: "For every complex problem there is an answer that is clear, simple, and wrong."

By design and in the name of efficiency, traditional hierarchies are intentionally exclusive and inequitable. When one person sits at the top of an organization chart, by definition others are excluded or in lower or lesser positions, thus excluding them from the highest levels of decision making. Invitational theory (Purkey & Novak, 1996) suggests that being intentionally inviting creates a more inclusive environment. All too often, processes, policies, people, places, and programs are disinviting to those who traditionally have been excluded from power and decision making. So our charge is to create structures that invite participation so that those diverse perspectives can better inform and share influence in decision making.

Unfortunately, the structures that put an individual or a small group in charge of most decisions have limited the ability to learn and grow from diverse perspectives participating in identifying problems and designing solutions. We believe that the more people who are at the decision-making table and hosting their own tables, the better. Creating a climate that is intentionally inviting to a wide range of perspectives, experiences, and roles will help ensure that we create a more equitable and inclusive learning environment.

Emphasizing responsibility rather than role in a climate of shared influence is a mindset that intentionally invites people to the "deciding and doing" table. This approach is more inclusive and more likely to create an equitable learning *and leading* environment.

The shifts just described can be challenging to do well because they all are counter to what the accountability movement has valued. In addition, these shifts push on the behaviors and practices of educators—both teachers and administrators. Ultimately, these shifts are likely to create tension between a traditional approach to education that values rugged individuality, competition, and predictability because they emphasize collaboration, cooperation, and an innovation mindset. Yet they are crucial to continuous improvement and sustainable change, thus making them worth the challenge.

Building Leadership by Sharing Influence: MSLA

The Mathematics and Science Leadership Academy (MSLA) is situated in southwest Denver in a diverse neighborhood known for both its Latinx (mostly Mexican) and Asian (mostly Vietnamese) cultures. These cultures are rich and deeply embedded in the identity of the area and its residents. Most of the students are English learners and qualify for free or reduced-price lunches, creating an opportunity to implement practices that support language development by tapping into the cultural resources in the area. The school was designed to attract and retain highly accomplished educators who have the knowledge and skills to leverage these rich resources to enhance student learning. Here is where growing leadership becomes deeply important to the MSLA model.

The Mathematics and Science Leadership Academy was designed around a core belief that everyone in the school community is responsible for being a learner, a teacher, and a leader and that implementing a program aligned to that core belief would best serve the diverse students of the surrounding neighborhood. More than a decade into the school's existence, this guiding concept remains part of the core identity of the MSLA community. In this model, the formal leaders teach on a regular basis, the teachers engage in leadership of the school in both formal and informal roles, and the students are engaged in teaching and leading as part of the many opportunities available to them.

Networking Teacher Practice to Drive School Outcomes

Attracting accomplished teachers requires a climate that supports their ongoing growth as both teachers and leaders. With this in mind, peer observation and feedback were built into the design of the school and have continued throughout its existence. Although the form and structure have evolved over time, the basic concept persists: that teachers influence the practices of teaching and leading by learning from and with one another. In MSLA's early years, teachers would meet before an observation to identify what they wanted observers to look for related to their formal observation tool.

The school hired substitutes to rotate through classes so that 45- to 60-minute observations could take place. Then the teachers would meet to discuss what they observed—both strengths and opportunities for growth. Peer observation and feedback cycles have continued through school leadership changes and now include observations via video recordings that the observed teacher collects and discusses with his or her colleague. As a result, teaching and leading practices continue to be strengthened.

Embracing Dynamic Spheres of Influence

Teaching and leading are de-siloed at MSLA and illustrate one of the powerful ways the dynamic spheres of influence can inform and drive school success. The school's two lead teachers teach on a regular basis, and all teachers hold some level of decision-making responsibility for leadership via the team and committee structures. In this way, the school has developed a culture of collective leadership that includes a strong sense of shared influence and collective ownership of results.

Over the years, the school has gone through several iterations of aligning leadership structures to the specific needs of its students and educators. Without an individual in the formal role of principal, staff have the flexibility to adjust roles and responsibilities that would normally "live" with that formal role. During the early years, the primary leadership teams were organized around Peer Review and Evaluation, Curriculum and Instruction, Culture and Climate, and Data. Over time, the team configuration has shifted, but the central idea of "Everyone as a learner, teacher, and leader" has remained.

Recently both formal and informal leadership opportunities have been evident throughout MSLA. For instance, rather than one formal leader, MSLA has a leadership team that is made up of five staff members (two lead teachers and three senior team leads). In addition, the school provides additional opportunities for everyone to lead by engaging staff, parents, and community members in a number of school teams and committees, including the following:

- Collaborative School Committee (CSC)—Made up of staff, parents, and community members who advise and decide on budgetary and policy matters.

- School Leadership Team (SLT)—Consults with the CSC and provides a place and space for senior team leads to have decision-making influence.
- Instructional Leadership Team (ILT)—Gauges the climate and culture of the school and coordinates across teams.
- Social Emotional Learning (SEL)—Implements restorative practices and has a mental health team, including a psychologist and a social worker.

Other teams include Science, Technology, Engineering, and Mathematics (STEM); Personnel; and Multi-Tiered System of Support (MTSS). Regardless of how teams are structured, what remains is ownership by the people who have the opportunity and authority to lead the doing and deciding to benefit all.

Creating a Culture of Inclusive Collaboration

A strong sense of shared influence at MSLA allows everyone in the school to shift their behaviors and practices to those of a leader because they hold responsibilities for identifying and addressing challenges. The structures that allow for shared influence are designed to be intentionally inviting to all stakeholders in the school community.

The team structures in place at MSLA create space for everyone to assume responsibility for doing and deciding how the school proceeds. The team structure ensures that there are "seats" for everyone, and the staff intentionally invites individuals to occupy those seats. School staff host events that encourage attendance and active participation. For example, events are held in community spaces or outside the building rather than inside, which can put power dynamics into play. These events also always include several bilingual staff members who can translate information. In this way, not only are staff members intentionally invited into leadership, but so too are parents and caretakers.

The staff members at MSLA are able to actively and effectively engage in shared leadership because they have strengths in the conditions of capacity and resources (Chapter 4) and relationships and social norms (Chapter 5).

The school has built teachers' capacity to lead by engaging them in formal leadership roles via teams and committees and providing the resources of time and structures to engage in peer observations.

Strategies to Support the Shifts

Making the shift to responsibility instead of roles will require both technical and adaptive shifts, and attending to both is critical to success. Not only do we need to ensure that those taking on responsibilities for whole-school success have the technical resources they need (e.g., time, space, and opportunities to try and fail), but we also must provide the support needed to shift the behaviors and practices of those affected. Teachers frequently do not consider themselves leaders at the beginning of this work. On our annual surveys of collective leadership, this number has grown from 45 percent in 2018 to 67 percent in 2022 through the Collective Leadership Initiative in South Carolina. Similarly, the traditional role of administrator has been aligned with the identity of being "the" leader of a school. Even when administrators embrace a collective leadership approach, numerous pressures reinforce the idea that they *are* "the" leader. These behaviors and practices of teacher as follower and administrator as leader are deeply entrenched and must be explicitly attended to in order to experience sustainable change related to these shifts.

If you are curious about how your team is doing in this regard, ask yourself some of the following questions: *How often do educators have the opportunity to learn from and with one another? To what degree do educators have the opportunity to define and drive their own learning agenda? What structures are in place for educators to match their learning needs with other educators who have strengths in their area(s) of need?* The answers to these questions determine to what extent shared influence that leads to school improvement and better student outcomes exists in your school.

Now let's explore some ways to address both the technical and adaptive shifts needed to improve in this area. You can use the following strategies and tools to either initiate or strengthen your efforts to de-silo the practice of the adults in your school or district.

Strategy 1: Observe Leadership Practice

As Linda Darling Hammond and colleagues (2017) state, "high-performing schools—similar to high-performing businesses—organize people to take advantage of each other's knowledge and skills and create a set of common, coherent practices so that the whole is far greater than the sum of the parts." We encourage you to review the self-assessment on shared influence in Figure 6.3. This self-assessment will give you a sense of where your team is in regard to shared influence and is likely to generate ideas for how to strengthen this condition at your school or district.

Once you have completed the self-assessment, we encourage you to observe any practice of shared influence across roles and responsibilities and compare your assessment results with the evidence you saw. Engaging in self-assessment, observation, and feedback loops can de-silo the work and lead to learning that increases shared influence.

Lest you assume we are talking only about teachers observing teachers, or administrators observing teachers, we are not. Great value comes from administrators observing administrators, teachers observing or shadowing administrators, teachers shadowing students, educators shadowing support staff, and so on. This practice provides powerful insights into the ways that everyone in a school or district contributes to learning and well-being. Those who do this also gain empathy for their colleagues' challenges and successes and the ways in which their own behavior affects colleagues' work.

This is where all of the other conditions discussed thus far come into play. When everyone is clear on the vision and the strategy for getting to that vision, know they have the support of administration, are equipped with the resources they need, and have strong professional relationships, then aligned goals for learning and leadership will be a natural outcome. Educators will be able to articulate their learning needs and to trust that what the team is doing is on behalf of students and their learning.

The skills needed to engage with one another in peer observation, feedback, and learning are also some of those needed for educators to take on more significant leadership responsibilities. Understanding instructional and leadership strengths and how to leverage them for learning are key to the next strategy.

FIGURE 6.3

A Self-Assessment Tool for Shared Influence

Use this single-point rubric to assess where your team is with creating a culture of shared influence for collective leadership implementation. The target is in the middle column. Use the column on the left to identify where your team has fallen short of the criteria. Use the column on the right to record evidence that your team meets or exceeds the criteria.

Opportunities for Growth	Description of Criteria	Evidence of Success
	Shared work Educators (teachers and administrators) cocreate shared goals for both student performance and educator leadership. In addition, they have and use a system to track progress toward those goals. Educators (teacher and administrators) work shoulder to shoulder to identify and address challenges that arise with both learning and leadership.	
	Shared responsibility and decision making Codified and transparent structures are in place for shared decision making that leverages specific skills and expertise of teachers. Both formal and informal leaders have the autonomy to make some decisions that are beyond the confines of their classrooms and affect wholeschool success.	
	Reciprocal feedback Feedback processes are structured so that information flows in all directions (administrator to teacher, teacher to administrator, and teacher to teacher). There is a process to aggregate the feedback from all members of the team and take action in response to what is learned as a result.	
	Diversity, equity, and inclusion (DEI) Attention is paid to ensuring that people who represent diverse roles and perspectives share influence on school success.	

Strategy 2: Cultivate a System of Shared Influence

Adding to our understanding of the importance of shared influence, Jackson and Madsen (2005) observe that "empowered teams have proved useful for many organizations as they increase ownership, provide an opportunity for developing new skills, increase the overall interest in projects, and otherwise facilitate decision-making where the work is being done" (p. 1308).

The most powerful impact that focusing on responsibility instead of roles can have is to create more inclusive leadership—and therefore more shared influence—within a system that is not set up to do so. If we are going to create a more equitable learning environment, we must address this shortcoming.

Attending to domains of invitational theory (Purkey & Novak, 1996) is one approach that your team can use to design a more inclusive leadership system and decision-making structure. We suggest you start with asking yourself some of the following questions:

- **Processes:** What processes can we put in place to invite active engagement by those who may hold and contribute diverse perspectives? How might we make certain that team processes ensure that diverse perspectives are shared, heard, and considered in decision making?
- **Policies:** What policies are in place that may unintentionally disinvite diverse perspectives? How might those policies be adjusted so as to invite engagement? What policies may need to be created during the decision-making-team design phase to ensure inclusion and equity of input?
- **People:** How might you ensure that those people whose voices are traditionally underrepresented are included and have a sense of belonging on decision-making teams? What needs to happen so that everyone's voice has a place and space to contribute to the decision-making process?
- **Places:** What needs to happen to create an inviting and inclusive space for the teams to engage in their work? How might our working spaces be designed to be inclusive and encourage engagement and diverse perspectives?

- **Programs.** How do we ensure that our programs are enriching and inviting? What might we do to create engaging and interactive programming that invites all to share their perspectives?

Creating a climate of shared responsibility regardless of role takes more time, requires the rethinking of traditional structures, and relies on a number of skills that people in schools or districts may not be accustomed to having or using. Yet no priority can be higher than the promised payoff of a more equitable and inclusive school and system that better serves students, families, and communities. We cannot overstate the importance of this achievement. Our team believes, without a doubt, that we are always smarter together, especially when we invite diverse perspectives and include the voices of those who have historically been underrepresented. This belief is at the heart of our work in collective leadership.

Wayfinding Summary

Assuming responsibility for whole-school outcomes regardless of role is at the heart of collective leadership. It requires all colleagues—teachers and administrators alike—to share influence with one another for making decisions about the work and for doing the work. Completing the shifts described in this chapter relies on some strategies described in other chapters:

- Shared influence can thrive when administrators who hold formal and positional authority are willing to support the leadership efforts of others (Chapter 3), opening the door for collective leadership within their teams.
- Shared vision and strategy (Chapter 2) help to ensure that when educators influence one another, they are doing so in ways that align with the agreed-upon destination.
- Supportive social norms and working relationships (Chapter 5) create the foundation on which shared influence is built—influence that advances whole-school improvement.

7

Learning, Not Liability: Creating an Orientation Toward Meaningful Improvement

Several years ago, Ann and Alesha visited a K–12 agency with which we'd partnered on an ambitious project. During the meeting, the staffer responsible for leading the work had an "aha" moment about why a particularly thorny issue hadn't improved. She looked down as she apologized for not seeing and acting on a pattern that was suddenly visible as a result of the conversation: "That's a huge error on my part. I feel terrible."

Her supervisor spoke up: "No, that's not an error. You're experiencing learning. And that's what we do in education, isn't it?" The staffer agreed and after a minute said, "So, here's one idea. . . ."

As this conversation shows, admitting that we've missed the mark is never comfortable. Research suggests that doing so can affect confidence, disrupt our self-concept as competent people and professionals, and create a sense that we're losing control (Schumann & Dweck, 2014; Tavris & Aronson, 2007). When we avoid doing it in the context of our work as educators, however, we don't just avoid uncomfortable feelings. We miss the core of what it means to engage in and model teaching and learning. In the same way that we'd never berate students for admitting and correcting a mistake as they learn something new, we must never berate ourselves and our teams. And research shows that when we can admit what we don't know yet and are willing to rethink challenges, we become more effective problem solvers and build trust and leadership across our teams (Bryk & Schneider, 2002; Grant, 2021). With our agency partners, the conversation moved from realizing an issue to naming it and beginning to resolve it *together* in about three minutes.

This example illustrates why orientation toward improvement is a critical condition for both collective leadership *and* meaningful school improvement (Eckert, 2018, 2019). But it involves a delicate balance between our desire to manage risks and our desire to grow. How do we strike that balance and become, like the administrator we met with, able to turn challenges into opportunities through the work of learning?

Challenges and Shifts

Experiences with accountability systems, traditional power dynamics, and our own self-imposed pressures to serve others well when in leadership roles can dispose almost anyone to fixate on getting it "right" rather than making it better. But there are things we can do, as the agency partner we mentioned did, to spark orientation toward improvement within our teams. Our work suggests three critical leadership shifts that help schools go beyond compliance to access the work of meaningful improvement and innovation, which we define as generating fresh thinking that clarifies challenges, stimulates learning for professionals and students, and gets positive results (see Figure 7.1).

Before we unpack these shifts, let's address what we *don't* mean by them. *Success, compliance,* and *implementation* can be good and necessary things. Formal goals and directives are facts of work-life for anyone in education

FIGURE 7.1

Leadership Shifts for Orientation Toward Improvement

Moving from . . .	Shifting to . . .
Requiring success	Creating a brave space for failure and learning
Executing compliance	Inviting and engaging experimentation
Mandating implementation	Incentivizing change

(or in any field, for that matter). To some extent, every classroom and school is a point of implementation, and every local education agency and state agency is a compliance division. Ultimately, the shifts that create the condition of an orientation toward improvement are about the verbs. When we *require, execute,* and *mandate,* we ask our teams to repeat work exactly as laid out without thinking critically about whether those approaches really solve the problem we intend to solve and whether they may have unintended consequences.

Requiring Success → Creating a Brave Space for Failure and Learning

When we create space for raising questions about whether current approaches actually solve a problem and about possible unintended consequences—and then engage and encourage processes for teams to answer those questions—we are tapping into varied perspectives on root causes of the problems. Doing so can make us more likely to solve today's challenge and be one step ahead of tomorrow's. It also helps us adapt best and promising practice solutions successfully to our specific situation; "what works" depends on a host of factors, from learning styles to cultural context to the experience levels of the educators putting practices in place.

Decades of research tells us that honoring and engaging the professional judgment of our staffs makes it more likely that they'll feel supported, be satisfied with their work, and be retained over time. One essential practice here is thinking through how every leader in our teams (and especially those who are administrators or who hold other positions of authority) communicates expectations and desires for how work ends. When a team's work doesn't measure up to expectations—when it "fails"—it is often precisely because we have different ideas about what success would have looked like. That is why this book focuses first, in Chapter 2, on how we can shift our leadership practices on developing shared vision and strategy.

Additionally, if success is *always* required, we usually set teams up not for high expectations but for a lack of intellectual honesty about what's working and not working. Chapter 3 contains specific recommendations for administrators and others in formal leadership positions. The remainder of this chapter explores specific shifts in communication practices that can support your team in creating this brave space for learning and improvement.

Executing Compliance → Inviting and Engaging Experimentation

Creating an orientation toward improvement ultimately means that we still *reach* for successful implementation of ideas that meet our goals. However, we foster habits of mind—in ourselves and our teams—that encourage us to think more like the knowledge workers we are and less like factory workers in outdated models of rote, drill-based learning. An orientation toward improvement allows us and our teams to satisfy the changing conditions and requirements we can't choose, keeping our eyes and minds open to new opportunities that make our schools more equitable, curious, innovative places.

If that seems easier said than done, you're right. Feeling overwhelmed is a real factor in a profession where 70 percent of teachers report extreme stress, and 75 percent of principals reported (even before the pandemic) that their jobs have become too complex to be done well (MetLife, 2013). Some question whether real impact is beyond the control of their one team, school, or department. And even those who may *want* and feel ready to take on innovative work may hesitate lest they be seen not to comply with or prioritize policies and mandates. That's why we consider supportive administration (Chapter 3) to be the threshold condition for collective leadership and real innovation in schools, and why capacity and resources (Chapter 4) such as time are essential.

Mandating Implementation → Incentivizing Change

Let's say we've addressed the conditions just mentioned to the best of our ability and we know innovative work is possible. We still have to bring others along with us to create the *will* for change. Shifting our own and others' mindsets and behaviors can run up against much of what's been drilled into us throughout our careers—and even disrupt assumptions about schooling that we developed when we were students ourselves. Even so, most educators are in schools for the right reasons: because they want to make a difference for young people and believe schools are important in making that possible.

That shared value is what makes the risks and shifts doable over time, if not easily or immediately. Much of the rest of this chapter is devoted to walking you through a series of strategies to create an orientation toward improvement with your team. But first, let's look at how these challenges and shifts have played out for one school we've supported—a school that, perhaps like schools in which you've worked, was caught between the pressures of accountability goals and the need to serve students in deeper ways.

Learning to Risk, Gaining Control: Whitman Elementary

Whitman Elementary sits between a neighborhood with boarded-up homes and a whimsical park surrounded by wind-driven sculptures made from old farm machinery. This small town in North Carolina is both a struggling post-industrial community seeking new economic outlets and an emerging bedroom community for professionals and the creative class. Whitman's students and families aren't yet part of that emergence. Ninety-eight percent are eligible for free meals, and grade-level proficiency scores hover between 20 and 30 percent in math and reading.

But the school has been focused on preparing students for a future in the new community. Jobs in health care, financial services, government (including in the state capital, 40 miles away), and high-tech manufacturing will require problem-solving skills and STEM knowledge. Many teachers still taught the "three Rs," so starting in 2017, the school joined an inquiry-based-teaching network to support its teachers in learning instructional approaches for the "four Cs" of *critical thinking, collaboration, communication,* and *creativity.*

The problem was that persuading teachers to shift their practice involved taking on the risks of change as they developed the four Cs among themselves. So two years later, inquiry-based instruction was still happening only occasionally and in a few classrooms. Inquiry required taking the risk of making teaching less teacher-centered, and with accountability scores on the line, risks were often the last thing staff wanted to take. The school's leadership team also wondered if staff members were ready to take those risks. Would teachers have sufficient knowledge about inquiry-based instruction to design their own activities? Would they get discouraged if a first attempt at a student-centered learning experience looked less organized or sounded louder than what they usually saw in their classrooms?

But the school's leadership team—a STEM specialist, an instructional coach, and the principal—knew that staff's hesitance was grounded in concern for what was best for students and leveraged that to create a shift. Starting in the fall, they identified a handful of teachers who were already excited about the shifts and organized a "coding night" to showcase inquiry-based learning. Rather than trying to promote it among not-yet-engaged staff and parents, they promoted it to *students*—and the children's excitement became infectious. Instead of the usual turnout of a dozen or so families, parents and caregivers of 155 students were present, representing about half the school. Even the most skeptical staff members took notice, with planning for the next showcase event—a Dr. Seuss–themed literacy and STEM night—taking over staff meetings.

Turning over the planning and leadership of that event to teachers who'd stayed on the sidelines of previous change efforts was also a risk. The leadership team managed that by providing a clear vision for success (targets for attendance and examples of the types of activities that met the mark), coaching and facilitation support to ensure each staff member could meet that vision without stress, and embedding check-ins into staff meetings to promote transparent and collaborative planning without adding on planning time. District staff and community partners were also invited, raising the stakes but also building a sense of importance and excitement in being part of that risk together, as they sought to grow and improve the ways in which they served students.

The risks paid off against all three goals:

1. **Scaling the number of instructional staff leading and carrying out the planning, setup, and hosting of activities.** Two-thirds of staff were involved in planning at least one successful component and continued follow-up in classrooms.

2. **Integrating literacy and arts with STEM so an inquiry-based approach could carry across the curriculum.** Teachers proactively

and immediately initiated planning for classroom activities that carried inquiry-based approaches forward from a one-off event to daily instruction.

3. **Sustaining a high level of parent/family engagement, with at least 100 students' families consistently involved.** Attendance at this event grew to 300 participating parents and caregivers. Although the pandemic hampered follow-up in some aspects, the school team reported ongoing higher levels of communication between school and home during the early, chaotic months of the shutdown in spring 2020—a definite improvement from pre-pandemic, pre-inquiry times.

As the principal told us later, "As a principal, everything comes back to me. It's tempting to want to be 'in control.' It's a risk not to be; but you know, I can't be in every classroom anyway. That space is what gives teachers an opportunity to teach and learners an opportunity to learn. So my job is to help everyone risk in a safe way."

Strategies to Support the Shifts

Communication across our teams is not only strategically important but can be deeply personal as well. The strategic shifts we recommend for leadership practice here invite you and your team to reflect deeply on the smallest and most immediate units of what you do in leadership work, which can free up your team to have broader impact.

Strategy 1: Refresh Language for Improvement

Words matter. Cognitive scientists, communications experts—and anyone who's had hurt feelings after an exchange with a supervisor or a friend or loved one—can attest that word choice frames how we think about ourselves, our value to a team or community, and our ability to make a change. Language provides clarity about what we intend change to look like or obscures it. And it can engage others emotionally in ways that connect to their core values as people and professionals, or it can leave them feeling that the need for change is less urgent and important. (For more on why and how framing matters to engage others as willing agents of changes you seek,

Chip and Dan Heath's *Switch: How to Change Things When Change Is Hard* is a helpful, accessible, and even fun read.)

When we begin to talk about needs for change—and willingness to accept risk in order to learn, improve, and innovate—the words we choose need to create clarity and emotional engagement. Unfortunately, most words we have traditionally used to describe work in this space create either one or the other, not both. Let's look at what happens when the language of improvement bids for one of those to the exclusion of the other.

- **All emotion, no clarity.** If a school has a toxic culture and significantly lower than average results, most staff, students, and families would agree the school needs something deeper than mere *improvement*. Terms such as *turnaround* and *transformation* were developed to evoke a genuinely desired shift in direction and a process that addresses more than surface-level challenges. Here's the trick: although those words *sound* supportive and open-ended, they were used to refer to changes that emphasized compliance and consequences. Educators in many roles, from the school board to the whiteboard, sensed the discrepancy— a lack of clarity and alignment in meaning that undercut the attempt to emphasize emotional connection with the work of transformational change in schools. As a result, those words (and others like them) became ominous "newspeak" punchlines.

- **All clarity, no emotion.** Likewise, accountability policies lean heavily on the use of data to ensure that schools' results, and their growth and improvement, are equitable. That aim is both laudable and widely held by educators. But most educators do *not* primarily think of themselves as data analysts. They think of themselves as supporters, coaches, and shapers of others' learning. We would argue that this work requires constant if informal mixed-methods analysis. Terms such as *data* or *improvement science* are intended to signal what educators are being asked to lean into within their practice. However, they can instead serve to make the work of improvement *feel* like another discipline and therefore less accessible to educators without extensive technical training.

In our work with schools and districts, we have made some adjustments to our own language in order to rebalance clarity and emotion, and to build broader collective engagement with the work of change leadership. The replacement terms in Figure 7.2 can serve as a starting point for your efforts in this area.

As you read our starter glossary, you may have mentally added to the list of words you (or your team) would prefer never to hear again. This exercise

FIGURE 7.2

Reframing the Language of Improvement

Instead of . . .	Try . . .	Because . . .
Data	*Evidence*	*Data* typically is interpreted as a summative, quantitative result, whereas *evidence* considers formative and qualitative sources.
Improvement plan	*Action plan*	*Action plan* aligns thinking with *action research*, suggesting educator-framed and -led experimentation that flexes around student needs, rather than a formal document filed with the district or state.
Evaluation	*Impact assessment*	*Impact assessment* de-emphasizes formal research expertise or summative judgments about the quality or value of work, favoring ongoing consideration of a number of impacts a team's collective work might have over time.
Fidelity	*Follow-through*	The shift to *follow-through* aims to decentralize rigid implementation of a received solution, especially if part of what is discovered in impact assessment is that the solution or program isn't aligned well with actual needs. *Follow-through* simply suggests the team keeps its commitments to action, learning, and adjustment where needed to achieve goals.
Measurement	*Observation*	We definitely want to know that efforts have an impact on learning and other changes our schools need. Like *data*, the term *measurement* can place extra emphasis on quantifiable results. If we're building culture for our classrooms or teams, though, there might be other ways to capture results: observing engagement among students, perceived positive emotion in classroom interactions, and so on.
Distributed leadership	*Collective leadership*	*Distributed leadership* was intended to evoke a sense of shared participation in the work of leading schools. But it still requires someone to do the distributing, implying that there remains a person (or people) with ultimate power over all aspects of the schools. *Collective* implies that multiple people can and will be involved in all decision points so they reflect the best professional judgment of a staff with varied expertise and viewpoints on what students need.

can be a great activity to do with your school or district team to build a common language for the kind of meaningful improvements you want to create together. Additionally, the process of exploring the dreads and fears that these terms can evoke can help make light of them and release their hold on our thinking about what it means to risk, learn, and improve. Try the following protocol to build a new glossary with your team in as little as 30 minutes:

Begin the conversation (5–10 minutes)

- Frame the conversation with some version of the following. Make the phrasing sound like you and your team, but ensure that you use plural pronouns wherever possible to reinforce the shared nature of your intended work: *Language can often reinforce our mindsets and the way we do our work together. We want improvement and innovation work to go beyond just compliance and engage all the strengths of our team. So we want to be sure the way we talk about this work helps remind us of our intended approach.*
- As time permits, you can invite others to tell a short story about a time when language really affected their thinking about a particular effort or change. If you need to keep things lighter at first, encourage stories that might be outside a work context.

Generate "trigger words" that evoke compliance (5–10 minutes)

- Now invite the group to individually brainstorm words that reinforce compliance and accountability mindsets for them. If you are meeting in person, have them write words down on index cards or sticky notes (one word on each). For larger or virtual groups, you can anonymously generate these in a Google Doc or Padlet.
- If individuals finish before time is up, they can take time to review the group's work. If using sticky notes, "stack" common words.

Analyze (15–30 minutes)

- If desired, you can use dot voting or a quick poll to determine which words are most working against the mindset the group wants to create. Picking a "bottom three" or "bottom five" can be a great starting point while limiting time spent on the activity.

- Call for discussion of each: *What mindset might this word or phrase evoke? How might that work against the innovation mindset we want to create across our team?* Add notes to the "because" column of Figure 7.2.
- Now call for suggestions for the opposite: *What's the word or phrase that would evoke an innovation mindset that could be used in place of the original?* Add the suggested replacement terms in the "try" column of the figure.

Plan your shifts and wrap up (5–10 minutes)

- Call for commitments: *What are some upcoming opportunities to practice these shifts in language? What will we do to reinforce use of words that support our innovation mindset?* You might settle on a code or signal to remind colleagues, use "buzzword bingo" cards to catch relapses in language in your meetings, post the glossary in your learning management system or staff meeting space, or try something else.
- Determine a time to revisit the glossary you've created. You may note at the end that the glossary will remain open for additional input after the session, or decide to revisit and build it out on some regular schedule (at least annually). Doing so is a good way to keep your language and culture responsive to your evolving work.

Strategy 2: Make Innovation Micro to Invite and Engage Experimentation

For most people, *innovation* carries a connotation of something new, groundbreaking, big-picture, and flexible. For many educators, that can make innovation and improvement feel inaccessible because so much of our work is bound by routines of budget deadlines, board agendas, school calendars, and bell schedules.

But that connotation is only half of what innovation really should be. None of us—not teachers, not principal supervisors, not superintendents or school administrators—has time for anything that doesn't help us accomplish key goals. For innovation to be worthwhile or even possible to fit into our daily routines, it has to work. That's why we say that innovation is defined by being not only *new* but *new and more effective*.

In other words, you and your team will not take up innovation at the expense of the essential tasks you need to accomplish. Rather, innovation is what will help you think and work differently so that you can get "unstuck" and get even better results—without greater investments of time or energy.

Earlier in the chapter we discussed several reasons educators might not engage in, or be willing to lead, improvement efforts. Feeling overwhelmed, issues with locus of control, and lack of psychological and career safety can all affect willingness to engage with innovation and improvement work. In our work with partners throughout preK–20 education, we've found that a key to overcoming these barriers is making the change feel *smaller* and thus easier to achieve. For those struggling with feeling overwhelmed, small shifts and learnings fold more easily into full days and can even be integrated with or traded off against other work they are already doing. For those wondering about how much is really in their locus of control, it helps to acknowledge that we can't control a whole district or initiative, but we *can* determine things about our own practice and how we contribute to those bigger efforts. And if we start small, we keep risks small—so if it doesn't go well, we haven't lost much.

That strategy is one that the Whitman Elementary team used: working gradually to shift practice, one element at a time. They never rolled out a requirement that all teachers adopt inquiry or mandated full-staff professional learning. Had they done so, in fact, they likely would have stoked resistance. Instead, they defined a clear problem of practice to guide their work, invited participation, built expertise, demonstrated results of small shifts, and let those results persuade others to join. Their success—and that of other teams that are able to start and sustain innovation—was in defining problems of practice that kept the work micro enough to feel and be doable. Figure 7.3 shows five main traps that they avoided as they crafted those focuses with their team, along with test questions to help you avoid each one.

Some teams—or others more advanced in their work on improvement and innovation—may like to use theories of action or logic models to help move their framing of the problem into a logical series of strategies and tactics to create the change they want to make. You may already have tools for this, or you can access support from Mira Education to assist you; some downloadable tools and guides are on our website (www.miraeducation.org), including

FIGURE 7.3

Traps and Test Questions for Making the Work Micro

Traps	Test Questions to Avoid the Traps
Locus of control: The problem you've identified isn't yours to solve.	Is this problem of practice one that's in our locus of control? Or is it related to *someone else's* practice? If the latter, shift your focus to something related to your own practice.
Example: "How can we ensure all students arrive at school on time?" Unless you're getting licenses yourselves and forcing all students to take the bus, student transportation is not fully in your control.	*Example: What you can do is explore ways to minimize the impact of staggered arrivals: "How might we adjust school and classroom routines to soften the effect of late arrivals on learning?"*
Locus of control: The problem is focused on the people rather than their practices.	Is this problem of practice focused on observable actions, behaviors, processes, or decision-making systems rather than on personal attributes or opinions?
Example: "How can we get all staff to value students from different backgrounds and identities?"	*Example: What can be addressed is how staff behaviors affect students' experience of being valued as whole people and learners: "How might we support staff in developing behaviors that express our district's values of equity and inclusion?"*
Overwhelm: The problem addresses symptoms that put you on an implementation merry-go-round every year.	Is this problem of practice framed as an underlying challenge that helps us reach a goal when it's resolved?
Example: "How can we hire more coaches next year?"	*Example: Maybe you do need to increase coaching capacity, but is hiring a patch or a long-term solution? Instead: "How might we build and sustain coaching capacity for schools in our area over the next three years?"*
Overwhelm: The problem is about how to implement additional solutions without taking any other to-dos off the table.	To what might you say "no" in order to say "yes" to this new idea?
Example: "How can we add an hour of professional learning weekly to teachers' schedules?"	*Example: Consider letting go of or merging any redundant processes and practices: "How might we repurpose existing team and department meeting time to support shared professional learning at least once a month?"*
Psychological safety: The problem is disconnected from formal school or district goals and requirements, or the goal of a change isn't clear.	How can you create the connection between your work on the things you can change to relate to broader goals and initiatives that matter in the system of which you're a part?
Example: "How can we continue using a prior curriculum our staff preferred after a change is mandated?"	*Example: What your team and district decision makers agree on is that you want the curriculum that's best for learning. Identify the specific components of the prior curriculum that accomplished that (not just familiarity), and see which might be adapted into the new curriculum.*

information about workshops and other learning experiences. However, it's not strictly necessary to use these formal approaches. The key is that your team is really clear about the snapshots of success you may expect to see at different points in your process. (See Chapter 2 for support in thinking through establishment of a clear goal to guide the work.)

Strategy 3: Grow Proof Points to Incentivize and Scale Change

One of the most common questions we get from leadership teams (and one of our favorites to address) is "How do we get buy-in for this change we need to make?" Our answer is simple: you don't. As we pointed out in the framing chapter about collective leadership, the aim is to *avoid* the need for buy-in by having everyone engaged in building up solutions together through the practice of collective leadership.

We've already established that while some members of your team will be early adopters, others may prefer to join the work later. They'll be overwhelmed, desiring to focus on what's comfortable and known, or wanting to keep a tight focus on what they alone can control. In general, we agree that early adopters (whoever they are) are often the right people to get things moving. They are deeply aligned with the potential for improvement, and that enthusiasm will help them persevere and become strong ambassadors for the work. (See "Cautionary Notes" for some cautions to keep in mind.)

Cautionary Notes

One hidden danger in relying on early adopters is that doing so can divide staff into two groups with value judgments attached to them. Notice the difference between common terms such as *innovator* and *early adopter* on the one hand and *resistor* and *old guard* on the other. That judgment works both ways; we've heard people describe early adopters as "the usual suspects" and worse. Schools need both change *and* consistency; innovation is both new *and* effective. So if you have tension between these two groups represented in your building or team, you don't have an uphill battle. You are actually ideally positioned for authentic innovation that balances these considerations.

We also add a watchful word here about other factors that can lead some individuals to be consistent early adopters—especially if you notice the "usuals" share characteristics. For instance, if your focus is on an equity and inclusion effort and the individuals involved happen to be mostly people who are of color or LGBTQ+, this should flag questions about whether those individuals feel welcomed to lead on other areas, whether this sends subtle signals about who on your team is responsible for addressing social justice questions, and whether this results in the very best thinking to address the challenges ahead. Ways to consider strengths-based composition of your leadership teams, and to address potential equity and inclusion issues in how people engage, are covered in Chapter 5.

How those "early adopter" individuals share the work matters to engagement and to understanding how well ideas actually work. Developing a common, brief story that connects your work with impact can build will to engage with and scale new approaches. The following guidelines can help make your story as effective as possible:

- **Be clear about the need or opportunity that is being addressed.** Even if colleagues disagree with your proposed plan, building common cause based on a specific need can bring this group together and energize those with whom you share your work. Start and end every conversation with this message, since it's the "why."

- **Identify what was needed to make a new solution successful.** You want to be clear about what led you to try what you are putting in place—but also that it is an experiment that is subject to change based on actual results and that you are open to additional ideas as others join and think through the work with the initial team.

- **Name the challenges that have already come up and how you've resolved them.** If change were easy, it would have been done a long time ago. Being candid about where the difficulties lie builds trust that you are operating based on problem solving, not just passion for a particular approach. Being clear about your resolution, and about data that confirms what has worked, builds confidence in the team's capacity.

- **Ask related, open-ended questions as you go.** Ask for your audience's help to refine and build out the work or to resolve a particularly sticky question you are wrestling with now. One question we find effective is "What are your pain points around this issue right now?" Asking this lifts up many perspectives on a challenge, allowing you to understand all the ways in which a problem is affecting students and educators. It also encourages those to whom you're speaking to imagine themselves as part of your problem-solving team, if only for a few minutes.

- **Hold more than one conversation.** Holding multiple conversations and offering multiple opportunities may build commitment over time. Doing so also ensures that those who need to be informed even if not directly involved—including superintendents, school board members, and others in formal authority—are kept up-to-date and can share the story of your innovation too.

In addition to these guidelines, you can use the tool in Figure 7.4 (and available at www.miraeducation.org in a larger printable format) to lead your team through a series of prompts to think about what matters most.

Wayfinding Summary

Communication is how we set the stage for the mindset shifts we describe in this chapter, and thus it is the first step in building an orientation toward improvement within a team. The chapters specified in the following list address approaches that align with or build on some of the activities described in this chapter:

- The story we told at the start of this chapter about a partner at a K–12 agency illustrates how essential it is for those in supervisory positions

FIGURE 7.4

A Tool for Finding Your Story

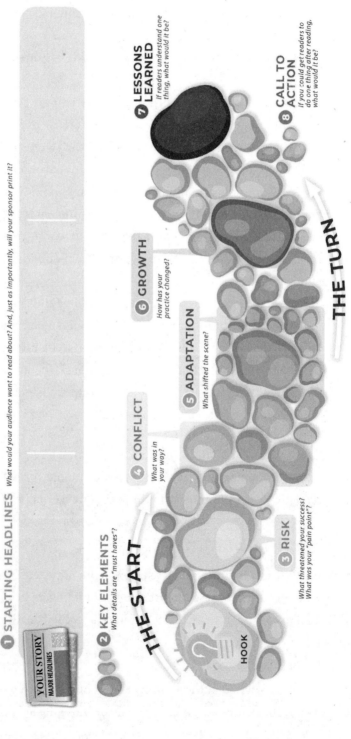

FIND YOUR STORY TOOL

MIRA EDUCATION

1 STARTING HEADLINES *What would your audience want to read about? And, just as importantly, will your sponsor print it?*

YOUR STORY
MAJOR HEADLINES

2 KEY ELEMENTS *What details are "must haves"?*

THE START

HOOK

3 RISK *What threatened your success? What was your "pain point"?*

4 CONFLICT *What was in your way?*

5 ADAPTATION *What shifted the scene?*

6 GROWTH *How has your practice changed?*

THE TURN

7 LESSONS LEARNED *If readers understand one thing, what would it be?*

8 CALL TO ACTION *If you could get readers to do one thing after reading, what would it be?*

to reinforce the first shift, from requiring success to creating a brave space for failure and learning from those moments. Supportive administration (Chapter 3) is essential to ensuring that space is explicitly set for the team.

- An understanding of working relationships and social norms (Chapter 5) helps us ensure that we communicate *with* and not *to* or *at* others, and that what we share reinforces the sort of collectively led team we seek to build.
- From there, all members of a team need to reinforce their shared influence (Chapter 6) on how the work of improvement is defined, designed, implemented, and sustained. Without such reinforcement, educators and teams will retain their orientation toward compliance with the perceived leader or manager, not their orientation toward improvement.

8

Aligned, Not Ad Hoc: Structuring Work Design to Support Sustainability

When you think about *sustainability*, what do you imagine? Maybe it looks like a project that your whole staff can get excited about and that you have adequate funding to support. Maybe it looks like effective instructional approaches or a school culture that won't be eroded by turnover. Maybe *sustainability* is as simple as ending every week energized by what your team accomplished instead of exhausted and headed toward leaving the profession yourself.

Whatever it is to you, sustainability in our schools and profession is more than a "nice to have." It's an essential. Meaningful school change and improvement efforts take from three to eight years to produce significant growth in student outcomes (Fullan, 2001)—and, of course, that's much more time than our school systems usually give curricula, initiatives, or frameworks an opportunity to work.

Typically, one of three reasons is given for lack of sustainability:

- **Time.** There wasn't enough time in the day or enough staff members available to dedicate their time to making a given effort work. Sometimes there wasn't sufficient ability to control how our time—or our team's time—was spent. Sometimes we simply overstuff schedules.

- **Staff will and capacity.** There wasn't sufficient funding to continue staff positions or professional learning experiences to ensure that the effort could continue or scale. Changing leadership can often be a factor in our capacity to support stable and harmonious priorities.
- **Fidelity.** No one could figure out how to implement the effort well year after year, so it was abandoned due to concerns about logistics or effectiveness.

These are all real constraints—and each of us has wrestled with them in our own schools and organizations as well as with our partners. We talk more about time and other resources in Chapter 4, about the role of administrators and in building will rather than buy-in in Chapter 3, and about building blocks for orienting your team toward improvement rather than lockstep implementation in Chapter 7.

Ultimately, however, sustainability relies on one thing: effectively structuring the work to hold up to the stresses of learning and change we've described throughout this book. Thoughtfully shifting how flows of communication, work, and decision making operate across your team makes changes more successful and more likely to stick (Campion et al., 2005; Hackman & Oldham, 1980; Margolis, 2012; Smylie & Denny, 1990).

Challenges and Shifts

Schedules and time management, professional development for educators, and careful attention to replicating success are cornerstones of practice for many of us. It might seem counterintuitive to make these shifts (shown in Figure 8.1), rather than pushing past the constraints on time, professional learning, and fidelity. The trouble with that approach is that "pushing past" rarely works in practice.

You may have seen your own experiences in the pain points we named at the start of the chapter. They also show up routinely in research on school change. Consider the following examples:

- Decades of surveys of U.S. educators in every role show shortages of time for focused instruction, for professional learning, and for data-informed

FIGURE 8.1
Leadership Shifts for Work Design

Moving from . . .	Shifting to . . .
Managing time	Managing focus and attention
Siloed professional development	Collective capacity building
Fidelity	Follow-through

planning and innovation (National Center for Education Statistics, 2012). Time shortages are seen to affect student learning, staff efficacy, and ultimately educator retention (Provasnik & Dorfman, 2005). These issues persist across school contexts but disproportionately affect schools serving largely communities of students of color, with low household incomes, or with more intensive learning needs.

- Professional learning is viewed as essential and is linked with improvements in teaching practice and student outcomes when it is contextual, job-embedded, and collaborative (Hill, 2007). However, many traditional professional development experiences fall short of that promise because they are too isolated from the act of teaching students and the context of working with a team of other educators to support those students.

- Fidelity is commonly used as a marker for effective implementation of new approaches, and we assume a dose-response relationship—that effects improve as fidelity increases. However, research suggests that is not always the case. As long as we have a baseline degree of consistency in implementation, there can be little benefit in moving from moderate- to high-fidelity efforts (Hill & Erickson, 2019). What may be more important is ensuring that aligned resources, work structures, and other supports are in place—and that educators are willing to engage in the change. The follow-through in lining up those supports may thus be the most critical element in implementing any change process.

This evidence and our own experiences in the field show that the need for these shifts is deeply pragmatic. What makes them so challenging is that they are also deeply symbolic and personal. First, shifts in our work designs affect how we see ourselves and our teams. In education, as in many other professions, our assumptions about "what we do" and "what others on the team do" are closely related to our professional identity. Thus, any shift in workflows—from who participates in a certain type of meeting to how a given staff member's time is seen to be spent—shifts not only how strengths are being logically deployed but also assumptions about who individuals are within and for their school or team.

What's more, those versions of professional identity also come encoded with assumptions about power and authority: who has it and who has less, based on the work they accomplish, the conversations they take part in, and the decisions entrusted to them. Most schools and other education organizations have traditionally been organized as hierarchies, with those at the "top" of the organizational chart (principals, superintendents, directors, etc.) making decisions with the broadest impact and considered to have the most authority or power.

Yet it's important to remember that the structure of the profession has more than top-down dynamics. The generally flat structure of the profession—with the vast majority of educators serving in classroom-based roles focused primarily on direct student instruction and support—does not mean that teachers have no power in traditionally organized schools. On the contrary, teachers historically have had (and strenuously defended) a great deal of autonomy—at least within the sphere of their classrooms. Although that autonomy has declined markedly over the last few decades (National Center for Education Statistics, 2012), we probably all have overheard the call to "just close your door and teach." Although that expression represents withdrawal in the face of top-down influence, it is also an act of protecting autonomy: one's own professional power within a particular sphere. Sometimes that can result in more personalized and student-centered instruction or deep peer collaborations, and sometimes in missed opportunities for improvement, alignment, and broader exchange of expertise across a team.

The value of thoughtfully constructed work design is to balance all these dynamics. In a collectively led model they should make each individual's expertise more accessible to themselves and to others and make formal authority a tool that can be used for the common good of the school or team. The following text explains how the shifts accomplish that.

Managing Time → Managing Focus and Attention

We talk about how we "save," "spend," and "budget" time for a reason. Like allocation of other resources that we described in Chapter 4, the amount of time we have in a day is limited. Surveys of educators in every role demonstrate that there is never enough. But more time isn't always *better* time. For instance, spending an hour in a workshop or tutoring a student while we or others are distracted by other concerns is likely to have little effect on anyone's learning; that same hour can be a game changer if we approach it with intention and focus. Ultimately, we do better if we worry less about managing time—over which we have limited control anyway—and more about focus. Where we invest our attention during time spent in a specific setting or interaction powerfully reflects what we value and prioritize.

Siloed Professional Development → Collective Capacity Building

Traditionally, learning experiences for educators privilege development of discrete competencies for individual educators, based on the roles and context for their work. In other words, administrators, teachers, education support professionals, and so on, all receive separate training even when the trainings focus on the same thing. This approach supports role specialization and makes scheduling convenient. But it can also give very different mental frameworks and strategies to different groups, and it allows educators to practice solutions only with role-alikes rather than with the range of other educator roles they will actually encounter when doing the work in schools. When school staffs are asked to take on shared priorities or work that melds complex processes—such as implementing restorative justice practices or developing a new school improvement plan—they can get stuck for lack of common language and common entry points into the effort. In short, they're acting as component parts rather than as a well-oiled team. (See Chapter 6 for further discussion of ways to build shared influence across a team, so that strengths of varied roles and individuals can be maximized.)

Fidelity → Follow-Through

Once we've set direction and built capacity, we have to actually guide teams in doing the work. Traditionally, teams will often focus on fidelity at this stage, as a way of ensuring that improvement and innovation work lives up to the promise of a good plan and can scale well as others get involved. However, we question whether a singular focus on fidelity is the right one. (For a discussion of why lockstep implementation of ideas can actually break down effectiveness of work and teams—and strategies to address this specific challenge—see Chapter 7 on building orientation toward improvement.) To keep follow-through on the essentials balanced with strong communication about where efforts may be breaking down, teams need to facilitate clear and timely communication across silos and stakeholder groups within schools and organizations.

We've briefly referenced how these shifts play out in supporting instructional change, professional learning for instructional staff, and other efforts that immediately affect teaching and learning. But as the following example shows, they also apply to broader change efforts, including shifting how key leaders within and across a district or an agency interact to ensure coherence, collaboration, and collective impact.

Creating Design That Supports the Shifts: An Urban Teacher Advisory Council

Work and interactions among teachers, building administrators, and central office staff are often structured through two channels: management strategies and (where they exist) bargaining processes. These structures can be helpful for monitoring progress of teams and individuals, ensuring compliance with key policies, and balancing power in decision making. However, the uneven power dynamics inherent in each can make it easier for concerns to escalate into conflicts between siloed groups. Participants in these structures, then, can be tempted to spend the majority of their time and energy either managing those conflicts or trying to prevent them, rather than think-ing jointly and flexibly about how to resolve shared issues.

A large urban school district in the Pacific Northwest was no exception. When Mira Education launched its work in the metro area in the early 2010s, the district was undergoing a series of senior leadership transitions and starting implementation of a new teaching evaluation system that required renegotiation of their contract with the local union. As a result, both the management and bargaining structures for the school system were expe-riencing upheaval, and neither had much bandwidth for addressing other issues. That situation was a challenge for both the union and the district, which had each made significant concessions during the bargaining process. A lot was on the line, including state compliance for a complex urban district, the future of the individual leaders involved, and, of course, whether the system could actually support schools in improving instruction.

District and union leadership teams made two moves that shifted the focus of implementation. First, they looked at all the ways in which the new system might fail. They were candid about the limitations of any evaluation system to make a difference if it only raised flags about teaching effectiveness rather than helping educators use the relevant data to grow professionally.

Second, they acknowledged that the structures that created the system— management and bargaining—weren't sufficient to keep it running well or focus on instructional improvement as well as performance monitoring. They could leave the tough conversations to schools, but that created one-off rather than districtwide solutions. They could leave it to the usual union-district leadership meetings, but that kept conversations infused with tensions left over from the bargaining table.

Instead, they convened a new structure: a Teacher Advisory Council (TAC) that engaged a districtwide group of educators to study the real impli-cations of new policies on retention, student learning, and school cultures. With support from Mira Education, the district and union designed the TAC to address potential failure points. To ensure that the TAC wouldn't be an extension of a bargaining table and could stay tight on problems but flex-ible on solutions, members were selected based on an application process that considered their ability to see a broader perspective, to engage rather than advocate, and to have trust from both peers and administrators. The pool was further balanced by experience level, race, gender, content area, grade levels, and district area. To ensure that the process felt fair to existing power structures but was grounded in school-based educators' work, a teacher leader was named to lead recruitment and facilitation, and both the union and the district had roles in selecting members from the pool assembled by Mira Education. To ensure sustained effort on the work rather than intermittent participation, TAC members received stipends and release time. To avoid conversations becoming siloed as a "teacher-only problem," school-based administrators and district and union leadership were invited into work sessions to join in finding solutions. Third-party facilitation and explicit framing of the TAC as a "third thing"—connected with but separate from bargaining and district management structures—also supported a focus on solutions rather than reinforcing the usual labor-management or teacher-administrator exchanges.

The TAC's work lifted up key considerations about limited time afforded to educators for work that didn't involve student contact. Planning, data analysis, collaboration, and professional learning were all essential if evaluation results were to inform instructional improvement. The TAC members, union leaders, and district administrators studied research on options for organizing schedules to maximize educators' focus rather than using all non-instructional time for administrative tasks, including reviewing best practices from leading global systems. They held conversations with peers to document the impacts of existing practices and developed a range of recommendations on which the district's schools could draw to keep efforts aligned without rigidly imposing yet another set of things to implement. These efforts did not (and were not intended to) stifle concerns about the new evaluation system. But they did ensure that it would be reframed as a strategy for improvement, not just compliance, and that there would be structured spaces in which concerns could be resolved.

The TAC itself faced challenges, including its own survival as leadership of union and district changed. The loss of effective work structures like the TAC due to transitions of key staff is all too common. Without approval of those with formal authority on an organizational chart, it is difficult to engage more professionals in the work of leadership. For this reason, we refer to supportive administration as the "threshold condition" for collective leadership. See Chapter 3 for more information and descriptions of related shifts and strategies. However, the TAC remains a strong example of how the three shifts—managing focus rather than time, de-siloing professional development to build collective capacity building, and supporting follow-through—can get effective changes off the ground. Moreover, its influence remains in how involved educators learned to build structures that create shared responsibility for identifying and solving problems. Those tools now inform their work in other regional districts, in state-level education initiatives, and in equity and diversity programs in the district and union.

Strategies to Support the Shifts

Again, we acknowledge that the looming factor in sustainability is often politics associated with the support (or lack of support) from key administrators or others with formal authority. Tools shared in Chapter 3 can help you address this threshold condition to get efforts moving. But once you do, you'll need to employ the other shifts to make changes stick and have impact.

Strategy 1: Analyze the Current Use of Time

Earlier in the chapter we described how "time shortages" are actually "focus shortages." When we look at a master schedule or at the schedule of an individual educator or student, we commonly see large blocks of time marked off for instruction or planning. But the questions to ask, as the TAC did, are whether that time is actually dedicated to those purposes and whether certain intended goals or focuses don't yet have dedicated time at all.

The first step in determining the shifts needed in how time and schedules are structured is to determine how time is currently being used. Depending on the tool selected, the data collected allow capture of the extent to which *scheduled* time remains *focused* time for teachers, administrators, and staff in other educational organizations. We suggest collecting over several days to gain a better understanding of the ways in which time is spent throughout the day. Figure 8.2 is a sample form for tracking, in 15-minute intervals, how time is spent in a classroom.

FIGURE 8.2

Time Trackers

It is important for you to create clear, appropriate headers for each column. Be as specific as possible to drill down to how your use of time aligns with your primary role, responsibilities, and goals. See the sample below.

Time	Whole-group Instruction	Small-group Instruction	Planning	Meetings	Emails/ Paperwork	Managing Classroom (discipline)	Handle Unplanned Business	Other
15 min.	X							
15 min.		X						
15 min.		X						
15 min. (HR 1)	X							
15 min.	X							
15 min.								
15 min.			X					
15 min. (HR 2)	X							
15 min.	X							
15 min.			X					
15 min.			X					
15 min. (HR 3)							X	

(continued)

FIGURE 8.2
Time Trackers (Continued)

Time	Whole-group Instruction	Small-group Instruction	Planning	Meetings	Emails/ Paperwork	Managing Classroom (discipline)	Handle Unplanned Business	Other
15 min.		X						
15 min.		X						
15 min.		X						
15 min. (HR 4)				X				
15 min.				X				
15 min.							X	
15 min.							X	
15 min. (HR 5)								Lunch
15 min.								Lunch
15 min.	X							
15 min.						X		
15 min. (HR 6)						X		
Totals	90 min.	75 min.	45 min.	30 min.	0 min.	30 min.	45 min.	30 min.

Copyright 2023 by Mira Education.

Once your team has collected data over several days, compile it for review. Consider the following:

- How much time was spent in each category? You might display this data as a pie chart that shows the "focus budget" for each area.
- As you analyze the larger areas of focus displayed on your chart, to what extent do they align with the intent for how time was scheduled?
- What areas of focus or work may not be represented sufficiently or at all?
- What might be opportunities to rebalance focus to align well with goals? Consider schedule adjustments, strategies to reduce interruption, or reassignment of work across a team to allow for stronger focus on core goals and improvements.

Assessing Your Competency

Microcredentials are competency-based assessments of specific skills. To earn microcredentials, educators submit evidence that demonstrates their ability to effectively implement a specific skill.

Mira Education has developed several microcredentials for collective leadership, including one, Assessing How Time Is Currently Used, that aligns with the process outlined here. To learn more and connect with partners who issue this microcredential, visit www.miraeducation.org.

Strategy 2: De-Silo Capacity and Follow-Through

You and your team have now considered how you're individually and collectively allocating your attention and focus. Next you need to determine the best ways to channel them going forward.

As with the TAC and many other teams described in case studies throughout the book, building teams aligned to the work at hand is a critical step to spark collective learning, leadership, and action on that work. The planning protocol in Figure 8.3 can help you map needs and construct teams

FIGURE 8.3

A Tool for Mapping Needs and Constructing Teams

Guiding Questions	Specific Needs	Related Criteria for Individuals in an Ideal Team	Considerations for Equity, Diversity, and Balanced Perspective
What is the work to be done? Describe the tasks and strategies that are part of the initiative or effort ahead.			
What concerns might you have about ways this work might fail?			
What are some opportunities that might arise in the work?			

around them. Start by responding to each question in the first column. In your responses, recorded in the second column, be as specific as possible about the needs of the work. In one district, for instance, they noted specific needs that led them to design a new structure for problem solving, as well as concerns about losing control of a process outside usual structures. Next, address these needs point by point in the third column. What knowledge, skill sets, mindsets, or other qualities might respond to needs and concerns or assist in taking advantage of opportunities? Again, be specific. These qualities form your skills-based selection criteria on which you'll build your team. Then, review these criteria to ensure they address balanced voice, participation, and power dynamics. Use the far-right column to make notes about decisions here, using the following questions as a guide:

- What additional criteria will help you hold yourself accountable to your equity commitments to your school or organization?
- To what extent are educators and staff in all affected roles represented in the work and learning ahead? (In one district, changes involved all educators at the school level, so they ensured that the team involved a representative sample across all educator demographics. Yours may be similarly broad; more targeted efforts, such as changing how beginning teachers are mentored, could allow for narrower criteria.)

- Depending on the nature of the change effort, to what extent are non–staff members (students, caregivers and parents, community members, policymakers) represented?
- For those not directly affected by a change, which individuals or groups may need to be kept informed or to approve? Note how you'll engage with them.
- What will you do to ensure that individuals meeting these criteria are actually selected to join the work and not just in the pool? Your list of concerns may influence thinking here. For instance, there was concern that TAC members might begin the work but then grow inactive due to busy schedules. Stipends and release time helped address those concerns.

Wayfinding Summary

Effectively structuring work for sustainability is no small feat. When we make shifts in how we *do* work and teams, we consequently shift how we *view* work and teams. Otherwise those shifts become disconnected and are not sustained. Time and continuing focus determine whether sustainability is realized. The chapters specified in the following list also explore aspects of these shifts:

- Work design for your team is all about how your time and energy are being spent. Consider these as the most critical of your resources (Chapter 4) as you think about what shifts are necessary and possible to completely leverage the expertise and leadership within the team.
- Shifting our working roles and responsibilities will also shift our working relationships and social norms (Chapter 5). Considering these in tandem will make our work more effective, sustainable, and humane.
- Practices need to be revisited for results and redefined when those results fall short, but the most daunting step may be the first one: getting started. We offer up some encouragement in how to do so as we conclude with Chapter 9.

9

A Call to Collective Action

Throughout this book, we have shared real stories about real educators who shifted how they lead, creating conditions for collective leadership, change, and impact. In each of the case stories, we have emphasized one specific condition on which those educators focused so that we could illuminate the ways in which that condition can make a difference within a school or district.

But as you might guess, that choice of focus means we told just a slice of each story. In reality, the conditions operate much like members of teams: interdependently rather than in silos. This means that as we work on challenges in a school or district, we typically find ourselves looking at the *interplay* among several conditions.

Now let's look at a more complex story. As you read, consider where you see the seven conditions showing up in this school's work. If you were charged with supporting this team, where might you recommend they start?

Collaborative Complexity: One School's Problem of Practice

Community Campus was the picture of a thriving school. It supported a diverse group of students and families who were passionate about their neighborhood school. A consistent core of the staff remained in place year after year, and the school had a strong tradition of teacher leadership in place. Instruction was data-informed and creatively tailored to meet students' personalized learning needs, with a strong focus on challenge-based learning. Test scores generally met or exceeded proficiency goals, but the real success was in seeing students engaged and excited to be in their classrooms.

However, the staff worried—first privately, in before- and after-school conversations, and then very publicly in staff meetings—that Community might become a victim of its success. Originally, it had been a K–8 school, but its reputation caused booming enrollment in the early grades, necessitating a split into two campuses serving elementary and middle grades separately. Having more space was essential, but there were growing pains. For one thing, the kindergarten classrooms in the new K–4 building had been placed in a former middle-grades wing. The location gave easier access to the playground and specials classrooms, which teachers found convenient, but the setup required shorter students to use taller water fountains and bathrooms in their new space. Messes and falls from stepstools were common.

Physical distance also made it more difficult for the two groups of faculty to collaborate and communicate as organically as they once had. Without the ability to go back and forth among classrooms any time an idea or a question came up, educators weren't sure how to connect. As a result, student transitions across the two buildings were getting more difficult to navigate well, vertical planning rarely occurred, and the staff simply felt fractured, as if they taught in two separate schools rather than one.

The physical element wasn't the only divide among the school's educators. Longtime staff felt a great deal of responsibility for carrying on Community's culture, which had depended on that deep and constant collaboration. Unsure whether more recent colleagues could be ready so soon to share leadership—and viewing the split campuses as a threat to the school's focus and culture—those teachers doubled down on time spent in committees and working groups. Sometimes that invested time led to solutions, but it also meant that the teachers were overcommitted and at risk of burnout. Meanwhile, newer members of the team were less familiar with the "Community way" and sometimes felt alienated or unsure how to break through into the core group to share what they knew. "Sometimes," one said, "it seems like any new idea I have isn't seen as a new idea by some of the teachers who have been here longer. It's seen as a threat to the school."

The school's two assistant principals (one in each building) were part of the longtime group of teacher leaders. When the principal retired at the start of the school year, one of them had been named interim principal. As the search for a new principal dragged on, each of the assistant principals got pulled more deeply into issues pertaining to their specific buildings and into coverage of meetings at the district office. That left them little bandwidth to think about the bigger challenges that the staff faced. The situation nagged at them, but neither they nor others on the team could figure out where to begin.

Finding Your Own Starting Point

Throughout the book we have highlighted schools that engaged in processes and practices that worked well in their given context. What we did *not* do is hold any of them up as being *the* example. The schools and teams highlighted in this book are not perfect, and the educators who work there would be the first to let you know that. But they *are* always working on progress for their practice, which is why we chose to include them in Chapters 2 through 8.

We know that schools are dynamic, vibrant places where the context and situation change regularly. What works today, this week, or this year may not work tomorrow, next week, or next year because the situation and context can shift. The same is true for the schools whose stories we have shared. Some school teams have made steady progress as they continue to implement the leadership shifts described in this book and create the conditions for collective leadership to thrive. Others have seen ebbs and flows on their journey, with some even lapsing into old patterns because of changes in their context or situation. In the cases where progress has stalled or lapsed, teams recognize that has happened, recommit to the work, and get themselves back on the path to progress. At the end of the day, these school teams can still describe themselves as being collectively led because they show up each day with that intention.

Your team can do the same: position yourselves to show up with the intention to engage in collective leadership. So, where might you start in examining the story that surrounds you and your colleagues each day?

The good news is that there is no wrong answer. *Starting where you can, as soon as you can* is the right approach. Here are three ways you might identify your own best starting point:

- **Start with root cause.** Sometimes it's clear that one condition is most affecting the challenges your team faces. It might show up as a recurring issue or a theme across a number of areas of your work. That's a good sign that a particular condition is at the root of your challenge and should be your beginning focus. If you can resolve that root issue, many other matters may begin to resolve themselves.

- **Start from your strength.** The seven conditions are not an "all or nothing" proposition. Most schools have a blend of strength areas and stretch areas—just like the individual educators who make up their staff. Consider which conditions are your team's strengths and how those might be leveraged to support work on any of the conditions you want to improve. Choose the focus that plays to your current collective capacity.

- **Start with what's simple.** Sometimes momentum matters. You can keep this process radically simple by selecting a focus on which you can get a quick win. That experience will invite your team to focus on new ways of working together, celebrate a success, and then use the resulting energy and efficacy to tackle tougher challenges.

A Final Word About Making Commitments to Collective Leadership

We cannot emphasize enough that collective leadership is a process or practice and not a program. It is a different means by which to engage in work that is inclusive. And as a result of the inclusion of diverse perspectives, it is a more equitable means by which to accomplish the work of a school or district.

We offer three strategies for most effectively using the resources in this book:

- **Address one chapter or set of shifts at a time.** Don't try to do everything at once. The shifts in leadership practice described here require both technical and adaptive changes for you and your team. Allowing the time and space to do them well is what will best serve your team and the work you do together.
- **Keep in mind that small or micro shifts over time can lead to big results.** Some of our school examples include small shifts such as noticing and naming success stories and shifting how norms were developed. These small shifts resulted in significant impact.
- **Use the additional online materials** that are available on the Mira Education website (www.miraeducation.org), or contact us so that we can help serve as your design and implementation partner.

So what now? We invite your team to make three commitments to the work and to one another.

See your connections. No school's transformation relies on a single factor or condition. Although we highlighted just one from each profiled school for clarity in earlier chapters, we revisit some of those stories below to show the interplay among conditions and discuss how that informs ongoing use of the book to strengthen leadership practice. We only told you part of each school's story—successful episodes. As noted earlier, some of the schools have accelerated, some have struggled, but they keep going and working to improve.

In Chapter 4, we described Walker-Gamble Elementary in terms of resources and capacity, but that case study holds other stories. This example could just as easily be included in the chapter on supportive administration because the first-year principal decided to invest his time and personal development in collective leadership work as a strategy for improvement—a gamble that paid off. In addition, the story of this school could be in the chapter on shared influence because the superintendent's engagement in learning allowed her to connect differently with teachers in the building.

And from Chapter 2, the Illinois district case highlighted commitment to vision and strategy in the face of urgent needs for change, but supportive administration (Chapter 3) was necessary to engage coaches and teachers in new modes for hybrid teaching during the pandemic. In addition, relationships and social norms (Chapter 5) allowed for the building of trust and ensured that the superintendent and senior leadership could cultivate a culture focused on equity at every level of the district's structure. Furthermore, work structures permitted equity and leadership teams in the central office to collaborate seamlessly to support leaders/educators whom they each worked with, without creating silos of expertise.

Find your network. Networks provide opportunities for school teams to support and learn from one another. In our work with the Collective Leadership Initiative, we have seen the collective leadership practices of schools accelerate dramatically as a result of their involvement in a network. Not only do schools within the same cohort support and learn from one another, but the most dramatic acceleration and improvement in collective leadership practice take place when teams share *across* cohorts. We invite your team to "meet" highlighted schools and school leadership teams through audio and video interviews or to contact them directly to learn more and to tap into an already existing network, or to create one of your own.

Tell your story. Through networks and within your school or district, share successes and lessons learned. The process of sharing publicly transforms implicit learning into explicit knowledge that can inform and scale collective leadership.

Resources for Your Own Practice

As you consider the details of Community Campus, we encourage you to use the reinforcement/planning tool in Figure 9.1 to cite evidence of each of the seven conditions of collective leadership that emerge in that story. That practice run of analysis will better equip you to then assess your own work context to determine what might be your best starting point for shifts toward a more collectively led workplace.

FIGURE 9.1

A Tool for Reinforcement and Planning

Chapter	Condition	Evidence from Compiled Story	Our Context* (1 = Challenging; 2 = Developing; 3 = Effective; 4 = Strong)			
2	**Shared vision and strategy** for improvement and innovation are clearly defined, communicated, and used to guide work.		1	2	3	4
			Evidence:			
3	**Supportive administration** at all levels provides visible, formal support for collectively led efforts.		1	2	3	4
			Evidence:			
4	**Resources and capacity** such as existing staff, funds, physical space, and leadership expertise are allocated flexibly and effectively.		1	2	3	4
			Evidence:			
5	**Supportive social norms and working relationships** foster a trust-based, transparent culture.		1	2	3	4
			Evidence:			
6	**Shared influence** among formal and informal leaders allows people throughout the organization to decide and do.		1	2	3	4
			Evidence:			
7	**Orientation toward improvement** at all levels of the system supports inquiry and risk taking in the name of innovation and growth.		1	2	3	4
			Evidence:			
8	**Work design** supports collective efforts that allow staff to align schedules for regular collaboration, observations of one another's practice, and pursuit of shared innovation and leadership work.		1	2	3	4
			Evidence:			

* Self-assessment rubrics can be found at www.miraeducation.org/tools.

References

Alexander, D., Lewis, L., & Ralph, J. (2014). *Condition of America's public school facilities: 2012–13*. National Center for Education Statistics. https://nces.ed.gov/pubs2014/2014022.pdf

Baldoni, J. (2009, November 19). New study: How communication drives performance. *Harvard Business Review*. https://hbr.org/2009/11/new-study-how-communication-dr

Bill & Melinda Gates Foundation. (2014). *Teachers know best: Teachers' views on professional development*. https://s3.amazonaws.com/edtech-production/reports/Gates-PDMarketResearch -Dec5.pdf

Bleiberg, J., Brunner, E., Harbatkin, E., Kraft, M. A., & Springer, M. (2021). *The effect of teacher evaluation on achievement and attainment: Evidence from statewide reforms* (EdWorkingPaper: 21-496). Annenberg Institute for School Reform, Brown University.

Bolman, L. G., & Deal, T. E. (2017). *Reframing organizations: Artistry, choice, and leadership* (6th ed.). Jossey-Bass.

Branch, G. F., Hanushek, E. A., & Rivkin, S. G. (2012). *Estimating the effect of leaders on public sector productivity: The case of school principals*. National Bureau of Economic Research. http://www.nber.org/papers/w17803

Brown, B. (2018). *Dare to lead*. Random House.

Bryk, A. S., Gomez, L. M., Grunow, A., & LeMahieu, P. G. (2015). *Learning to improve: How America's schools can get better at getting better*. Harvard Education Press.

Bryk, A. S., & Schneider, B. (2002). *Trust in schools: A core resource for improvement*. Russell Sage Foundation.

Bryk, A. S., Sebring, P. B., Allensworth, E., Luppescu, S., & Easton, J. Q. (2010). *Organizing schools for improvement: Lessons from Chicago*. University of Chicago Press.

Campion, M. A., Mumford, T. V., Morgeson, F. P., & Nahrgang, J. D. (2005). Work redesign: Eight obstacles and opportunities. *Human Resource Management, 44*(4), 367–390.

Carver-Thomas, D., & Darling-Hammond, L. (2017). *Teacher turnover: Why it matters and what we can do about it*. Learning Policy Institute. https://learningpolicyinstitute.org/sites /default/files/product-files/Teacher_Turnover_REPORT.pdf

Carver-Thomas, D., & Darling-Hammond, L. (2019). The trouble with teacher turnover: How teacher attrition affects students and schools. *Education Policy Analysis Archives, 27*(36).

Cherry, K. (2020, September 18). How does implicit bias influence behavior? *Verywell Mind.* https://www.verywellmind.com/implicit-bias-overview-4178401

Clear, J. (2018). *Atomic habits: An easy and proven way to build good habits and break bad ones.* Avery.

Darling-Hammond, L., Burns, D., Campbell, C., Goodwin, A. L., Hammerness, K., Low, E. L., McIntyre, A., Sato, M., & Zeichner, K. (2017). *Empowered educators: How high-performing systems shape teaching quality around the world.* Jossey-Bass.

Day, D. V., Zaccaro, S. J., & Halpin, S. M. (2004). *Leader development for transforming organizations: Growing leaders for tomorrow.* Psychology Press.

Deci, E. L., & Flaste, R. (1995). *Why we do what we do: Understanding self-motivation.* Penguin.

DeMatthews, D. E., Kotok, S., & Serafini, A. (2020). Leadership preparation for special education and inclusive schools: Beliefs and recommendations from successful principals. *Journal of Research on Leadership Education, 15*(4), 303–329.

Dill, K. (2022, January 31). Teachers are quitting, and companies are hot to hire them. *Wall Street Journal.* https://www.wsj.com/articles/teachers-are-quitting-and-companies-are-hot-to-hire-them-11643634181

DiPaola, M. F., & Tschannen-Moran, M. (2005). Bridging or buffering?: The impact of schools' adaptive strategies on student achievement. *Journal of Educational Administration, 43*(1), 60–71.

Donohoo, J., Hattie, J., & Eells, R. (2018). The power of collective efficacy. *Educational Leadership, 75*(6), 40–44. https://www.ascd.org/el/articles/the-power-of-collective-efficacy

Duarte, N. (2020, May 6). Good leadership is about communicating "why." *Harvard Business Review.* https://hbr.org/2020/05/good-leadership-is-about-communicating-why

DuFour, R. (2004). What is a "professional learning community"? *Educational Leadership, 61*(8). https://www.ascd.org/el/articles/what-is-a-professional-learning-community

Duke, D. (2008, March). *How do you turn around a low-performing school?* ASCD Annual Conference, New Orleans, LA.

Eckert, J. (2016). *The novice advantage: Fearless practice for every teacher.* Corwin.

Eckert, J. (2017, September 13). The "no" in "innovate." *Edutopia.* https://www.edutopia.org/article/no-innovate/

Eckert, J. (2018). *Leading together: Teachers and administrators improving student outcomes.* Corwin.

Eckert, J. (2019). Collective leadership development: Emerging themes from urban, suburban, and rural high schools. *Educational Administration Quarterly, 55*(3), 477–509.

Eckert, J. (2020, July 16). 3 keys to a better 2020–21. *Edutopia.* https://www.edutopia.org/article/3-keys-better-2020-21

Eckert, J., & Butler, J. (2021). Teaching and leading for exemplary STEM learning. *The Elementary School Journal, 121*(4), 674–699.

Eckert, J., Cann, B., Rammer, B., & Schuler, J. (2018, September 17). How to build a better teacher contract. *Education Week.* https://www.edweek.org/teaching-learning/opinion-how-to-build-a-better-teacher-contract/2018/09

Eckert, J., & Daughtrey, A. (2018). *Conditions for teacher leadership: Findings from one district's implementation of Iowa's Teacher Leadership and Compensation System.* American Education Research Association, New York.

Ferillo, B. (2005). *Corridor of shame: The neglect of South Carolina's rural schools.* University of South Carolina Press.

Fullan, M. (2001). *Whole school reform: Problems and promises* [paper]. Chicago Community Trust.

Fullan, M. (2005). *Leadership and sustainability: System thinkers in action.* Corwin.

Gecker, J. (2021, September 22). COVID-19 creates dire US shortage of teachers, school staff. *U.S. News & World Report.* https://www.usnews.com/news/business/articles/2021-09-22/covid-19-creates-dire-us-shortage-of-teachers-school-staff

Goldhaber, D., Theobald, R., & Tien, C. (2020). *The theoretical and empirical arguments for diversifying the teacher workforce: A review of the evidence* [CEDR working paper]. Center for Education Data and Research.

Grant, A. (2021). *Think again: The power of knowing what you don't know.* Viking.

Hackman, J. R., & Oldham, G. R. (1980). *Work redesign.* Addison-Wesley.

Hanushek, E. A. (1992). The trade-off between child quantity and quality. *Journal of Political Economy, 100*(1), 84–117.

Hanushek, E. A., & Rivkin, S. G. (2012). The distribution of teacher quality and implications for policy. *Annual Review of Economics, 4,* 131–157.

Hargreaves, A., & Fink, D. (2006). *Sustainable leadership.* Jossey-Bass.

Hargreaves, A., & O'Connor, M. T. (2018). *Collaborative professionalism: When teaching together means learning for all.* Corwin.

Hattie, J. (2018). *Hattie ranking: 252 influences and effect sizes related to student achievement.* https://visible-learning.org/hattie-ranking-influences-effect-sizes-learning-achievement/

Heath, C., & Heath, D. (2017). *The power of moments: Why certain experiences have extraordinary impact.* Simon & Schuster.

Heifetz, R. A. (1994). *Leadership without easy answers.* Harvard University Press.

Hill, H. C. (2007). Learning in the teaching workforce. *Future of Children, 17*(1), 111–127.

Hill, H. C., & Erickson, A. (2019). Using implementation fidelity to aid in interpreting program impacts: A brief review. *Educational Researcher, 48*(9), 590–598.

Hong Bui, V. S. C., Degl'Innocenti, M., Leone, L., & Vicentini, F. (2019). The resilient organisation: A meta-analysis of the effect of communication on team diversity and team performance. *Applied Psychology, 68*(4), 621–657.

Jackson, B., & Madsen, S. (2005). Common factors of high performance teams. https://eric.ed.gov/?id=ED492231

Jackson, C. K., & Bruegmann, E. (2009). Teaching students and teaching each other: The importance of peer learning for teachers. *American Economic Journal: Applied Economics, 1*(4), 85–108.

Jackson, C. K., Johnson, R. C., & Persico, C. (2015). Boosting educational attainment and adult earnings. *Education Next, 15*(4). http://educationnext.org/boosting-education-attainment-adult-earnings-school-spending/

Johnson, S. M., Papay, J. P., Fiarman, S. E., Munger, M. S., & Quazilbash, E. K. (2010). *Teacher to teacher: Realizing the potential of peer assistance and review.* Center for American Progress. https://files.eric.ed.gov/fulltext/ED565879.pdf

Johnston, W. R., & Tsai, T. (2018). *The prevalence of collaboration among American teachers: National findings from the American teacher panel* [Research report]. RAND Corporation. https://www.rand.org/content/dam/rand/pubs/research_reports/RR2200/RR2217/RAND_RR2217.pdf

Jotkoff, E. (2022). *NEA survey: Massive staff shortages in schools leading to educator burnout; alarming number of educators indicating they plan to leave profession* [Press release]. NEA. https://www.nea.org/about-nea/media-center/press-releases/nea-survey-massive-staff-shortages-schools-leading-educator

Kamenetz, A. (2022, February 1). More than half of teachers are looking for the exits, a poll says. *NPR.* https://www.npr.org/2022/02/01/1076943883/teachers-quitting-burnout

Kane, T. J., & Staiger, D. O. (2008). *Estimating teacher impacts on student achievement: An experimental evaluation* [Working paper 14607]. National Bureau of Economic Research.

Kegan, R., & Lahey, L. L. (2009). *Immunity to change: How to overcome it and unlock the potential in yourself and your organization.* Harvard Business Press.

Kellerman, B. (2004). *Bad leadership: What it is, how it happens, why it matters.* Harvard Business School Press.

Kraft, M. A., & Papay, J. P. (2016). *Developing workplaces where teachers stay, improve, and succeed.* Albert Shanker Institute. https://www.shankerinstitute.org/blog/developing-workplaces-where-teachers-stay-improve-and-succeed

Lai, E., & Cheung, D. (2015). Enacting teacher leadership: The role of teachers in bringing about change. *Educational Management Administration & Leadership, 43*(5), 673–692.

Learning Policy Institute. (2018). *Understanding teacher shortages, 2018 update: A state-by-state analysis of the factors influencing teacher supply, demand, and equity.* https://learningpolicyinstitute.org/product/understanding-teacher-shortages-interactive?gclid=CjwKCAjwzvX7BRAeEiwAsXExo8uGleRNcplMt15XOzJr6GOakJ5zYNfENdy0ERUrLSb756YSmGvv4BoC124QAvD_BwE

Lee, M., Ryoo, J. H., & Walker, A. (2021). School principals' time use for interaction with individual students: Macro contexts, organizational conditions, and student outcomes. *American Journal of Education, 127*(2), 303–344.

Leithwood, K., & Louis, K. S. (2012). *Linking leadership to student learning.* Jossey-Bass.

Leithwood, K., Louis, K. S., Anderson, S., & Wahlstrom, K. (2004). *How leadership influences student learning.* Wallace Foundation.

Leithwood, K., & Mascall, B. (2008). Collective leadership effects on student achievement. *Educational Administration Quarterly, 44*(4), 529–561.

Light, P. C. (1998). *Sustaining innovation: Creating nonprofit and government organizations that innovate naturally.* Jossey-Bass.

Louis, K. S., Leithwood, K., Wahlstrom, K. L., & Anderson, S. E. (2010). *Investigating the links to improved student learning: Final report of research findings.* Wallace Foundation.

http://www.wallacefoundation.org/knowledge-center/Documents/Investigating-the-Links
-to-Improved-Student-Learning.pdf

Margolis, J. (2012). Hybrid teacher leaders and the new professional development ecology. *Professional Development in Education, 38*(2), 291–315.

McCauley, C. D. (2008). *Leader development: A review of research.* Center for Creative Leadership.

MetLife. (2013). *The MetLife survey of the American teacher: Challenges for school leadership.* MetLife.

Mira Education. (n.d.) *Collective leadership playbook: Vision and strategy self assessment.*

Muijs, D., & Harris, A. (2007). Teacher leadership in (in)action: Three case studies of contrasting schools. *Educational Management, Administration, and Leadership, 35*(1), 111–134.

Mumford, M. D., Hunter, S. T., Eubanks, D. L., Bedell, K. E., & Murphy, S. T. (2007). Developing leaders for creative efforts: A domain-based approach to leadership development. *Human Resource Management Review, 17*(4), 402–417.

National Center for Education Statistics. (2012). *School staffing survey.* https://nces.ed.gov /surveys/sass/tables/sass1112_20170808004_t1n.asp

Papay, J. P., & Johnson, S. M. (2012). Is PAR a good investment? Understanding the costs and benefits of teacher Peer Assistance and Review programs. *Educational Policy, 26*(5), 696–729.

Plecki, M., Alejano, C. R., Knapp, M. S., & Lochmiller, C. R. (2006). *Allocating resources and creating incentives to improve teaching and learning.* University of Washington, Center for the Study of Teaching and Policy. https://www.education.uw.edu/ctp/sites/default/files/ctpmail /PDFs/Resources-Oct30.pdf

Provasnik, S., & Dorfman, S. (2005). *Mobility in the teacher workforce* (NCES 2005-114). National Center for Education Statistics. https://nces.ed.gov/pubs2005/2005114.pdf

Purkey, W. W., & Novak, J. M. (1996). *Inviting school success: A self-concept approach to teaching, learning, and democratic process* (3rd ed.). Wadsworth.

Richey, M. (2020). *Future systems of learning and knowledge development: Human capital, sociotechnical systems and the flow of information.* Boeing. https://www.sri.com/wp-content /uploads/2020/08/NSF-08.06-2020-Future-of-Learning.pdf

Rivkin, S. G., Hanushek, E. A., & Kain, J. F. (2005). Teachers, schools, and academic achievement. *Econometrica, 73*(2), 417–458.

Ronfeldt, M., Farmer, S. O., McQueen, K., & Grissom, J. A. (2015). Teacher collaboration in instructional teams and student achievement. *American Educational Research Journal, 52*(3), 475–514.

Rosenholtz, S. J. (1989). *Teachers' workplace: The organizational context of schooling.* Teachers College Press.

Sanders, W. L., & Rivers, J. C. (1996). *Cumulative and residual effects of teachers on future student academic achievement: Research progress report.* University of Tennessee Value-Added Research and Assessment Center.

Schumann, K., & Dweck, C. S. (2014). Who accepts responsibility for their transgressions? *Personality and Social Psychology Bulletin, 40*(12), 1598–1610.

SC-Teacher. (2021). *Summary of results for the SC teacher exit survey from the 2020–21 pilot administration.* https://sc-teacher.org/wp-content/uploads/2021/09/SCTeacherExitSurvey _FINAL.pdf

Seligman, M. E. P. (2011). *Flourish: A visionary new understanding of happiness and well-being.* Free Press.

Smylie, M. A. (2010). *Continuous school improvement.* Corwin.

Smylie, M. A., & Denny, J. W. (1990). Teacher leadership: Tensions and ambiguities in organizational perspective. *Educational Administration Quarterly, 26*(3), 235–259.

Smylie, M. A., & Eckert, J. (2018). Beyond superheroes and advocacy: The pathway of teacher leadership development. *Educational Management Administration & Leadership, 46*(4), 556–577.

South Carolina Department of Education. (2016). *2016 SC school report cards.* https://ed.sc.gov/

Staats, C., Capatosto, K., Wright, R. A., & Contractor, D. (2015). *State of the science: Implicit bias review 2015.* Ohio State University, Kirwin Institute for the Study of Race and Ethnicity. https://kirwaninstitute.osu.edu/research/2015-state-science-implicit-bias-review

Tavris, C., & Aronson, E. (2007). *Mistakes were made (but not by me).* Houghton Mifflin Harcourt.

Van Velsor, E., & McCauley, C. D. (2004). *Our view of leadership development.* Jossey-Bass.

Waters, T., Marzano, R. J., & McNulty, B. (2003). *Balanced leadership: What 30 years of research tells us about the effect of leadership on student achievement.* Mid-continent Research for Education and Learning (McREL).

Wheatley, M. (2006). *Leadership and the new science: Discovering order in a chaotic world.* Berrett-Koehler.

Will, M. (2021, January 6). As teacher morale hits a new low, schools look for ways to give breaks, restoration. *Education Week.* https://www.edweek.org/leadership/as-teacher-morale-hits-a-new-low-schools-look-for-ways-to-give-breaks-restoration/2021/01

Wise, A. E. (2012, January 24). End the tyranny of the self-contained classroom. *Education Week.* https://www.edweek.org/teaching-learning/opinion-end-the-tyranny-of-the-self-contained-classroom/2012/01

Wiseman, L. (2017). *Multipliers: How the best leaders make everyone smarter.* Harper Business.

World Bank. (2020). *GDP ranking.* https://datacatalog.worldbank.org/dataset/gdp-ranking

Index

The letter *f* following a page number denotes a figure.

About the Authors

P. Ann Byrd serves as Executive Director and Lead Strategist for SC TEACHER, a research and resources initiative housed in the University of South Carolina's College of Education. Having formerly served the leadership team of Mira Education for 17 years, she continues to engage in efforts grounded in activating the collective power of educators to propel impact and advance the profession. In addition to 13 years of classroom teaching, she led work to recruit and retain teachers in positions with the Center for Educator Recruitment, Retention, and Advancement (CERRA). She served as a teacher in residence, program director, and then CERRA's executive director for six years, before joining Mira Education (then the Center for Teaching Quality, or CTQ) in 2006. She achieved National Board Certification in English Language Arts for Adolescents and Young Adults in 2000 (renewed in 2010) and also served six years as a member of the National Board for Professional Teaching Standards (NBPTS) board of directors. Ann holds a BA in English secondary education from the University of South Carolina (USC) and an MEd in English education from Winthrop University, as well as an EdD in curriculum and instruction from USC.

Alesha Daughtrey serves as President of Mira Education, accelerating partners' work to design, implement, and sustain strategies that build collective capacity in schools and P–20 education systems. Over the last 10 years, the team has supported more than 100 other leadership teams at the school, district, and state levels to craft teacher leadership systems, redesign supports for principals and leadership teams, improve professional learning and coaching, and develop effective and inclusive approaches to leading complex change. Before coming to Mira Education (then the Center for Teaching Quality, or CTQ), she served in a range of roles as a community organizer, grant maker, policy analyst, writer, and advocate, which continue to inform her approach to transforming education. Alesha holds a Master of Public Policy (MPP) degree from Duke University and earned a BA and initial teaching credential at the University of North Carolina at Greensboro.

Jonathan Eckert is the Lynda and Robert Copple Professor of Educational Leadership at Baylor University. Jon came to Baylor with more than two decades of experience in education, including 12 years of teaching near Chicago and Nashville. After completing his doctorate at Vanderbilt University in 2008, he was selected as a Teaching Ambassador Fellow at the U.S. Department of Education, where he worked in the Bush and Obama administrations on issues related to teaching quality. Previously, Jon was a professor at Wheaton College for 10 years. He is the author of *Just Teaching: Feedback, Engagement, and Well-Being for Each Student* and *Leading Together: Teachers and Principals Improving Student Outcomes*. Jon has also written and cowritten other books, numerous book chapters, peer-reviewed articles, and other papers that draw on his more than 10 years of collaborative research and evaluation work with the Center for Teaching Quality (now Mira Education).

Lori Nazareno is the Design Lead at Mira Education, engaging a range of partners to design and implement collective leadership in a variety of educational contexts. She is a former science teacher with 25 years of experience at the high school and elementary school levels. During this time, Lori led a team of educators that designed and launched a collectively led school in Denver that served some of the district's most historically underserved students and families. She has National Board Certification in Science for both Adolescents and Young Adults and Early Adolescents. She served six years as a member of the National Board for Professional Teaching Standards (NBPTS) board of directors, was a member of the National Education Association's (NEA's) Commission on Effective Teachers and Teaching, and served on the Teacher Advisory Council for the Bill and Melinda Gates Foundation. Lori earned a master's degree in sports medicine at the United States Sports Academy and a bachelor's degree in exercise science at Occidental College before entering the teaching profession through an alternative certification pathway.

Related ASCD Resources

At the time of publication, the following resources were available (ASCD stock numbers in parentheses).

Creating a Culture of Reflective Practice: Capacity-Building for Schoolwide Success by Pete Hall and Alisa Simeral (#117006)

Design Thinking for School Leaders: Five Roles and Mindsets That Ignite Positive Change by Alyssa Gallagher and Kami Thordarson (#118022)

Dream Team: A Practical Playbook to Help Innovative Educators Change Schools by Aaron Tait and Dave Faulkner (#119022)

Educator Bandwidth: How to Reclaim Your Energy, Passion, and Time by Jane A. G. Kise and Ann C. Holm (#122019)

Fighting for Change in Your School: How to Avoid Fads and Focus on Substance by Harvey Alvy (#117007)

Leading Change Together: Developing Educator Capacity Within Schools and Systems by Eleanor Drago-Severson and Jessica Blum-DeStefano (#117027)

Leading In Sync: Teacher Leaders and Principals Working Together for Student Learning by Jill Harrison Berg (#118021)

The Learning Leader: How to Focus School Improvement for Better Results, 2nd Edition by Douglas B. Reeves (#118003)

Make Teaching Sustainable: Six Shifts That Teachers Want and Students Need by Paul Emerich France (#123011)

The Principal as Chief Empathy Officer: Creating a Culture Where Everyone Grows by Thomas R. Hoerr (#122030)

Results Now 2.0: The Untapped Opportunities for Swift, Dramatic Gains in Achievement by Mike Schmoker (#123048)

Stop Leading, Start Building: Turn Your School into a Success Story with the People and Resources You Already Have by Robyn R. Jackson (#121025)

For up-to-date information about ASCD resources, go to www.ascd.org. You can search the complete archives of *Educational Leadership* at www.ascd.org/el. To contact us, send an email to member@ascd.org or call 1-800-933-2723 or 703-578-9600.

WHOLE CHILD
TENETS

1 **HEALTHY**
Each student enters school healthy and learns about and practices a healthy lifestyle.

2 **SAFE**
Each student learns in an environment that is physically and emotionally safe for students and adults.

3 **ENGAGED**
Each student is actively engaged in learning and is connected to the school and broader community.

4 **SUPPORTED**
Each student has access to personalized learning and is supported by qualified, caring adults.

5 **CHALLENGED**
Each student is challenged academically and prepared for success in college or further study and for employment and participation in a global environment.

**ascd
whole child**

The ASCD Whole Child approach is an effort to transition from a focus on narrowly defined academic achievement to one that promotes the long-term development and success of all children. Through this approach, ASCD supports educators, families, community members, and policymakers as they move from a vision about educating the whole child to sustainable, collaborative actions.

Small Shifts, Meaningful Improvement relates to the **supported** tenet.
For more about the ASCD Whole Child approach,
visit **www.ascd.org/wholechild.**